Enjoy garden-fresh foods throughout the year with a supply of canned fruits, vegetables, pickles, relishes, jams, and jellies. They'll be extra special when you can them yourself.

On the cover: Easy, yet elegant, best describes Cherries Jubilee. After the lights have been dimmed, the sauce is flamed at the table with brandy, then spooned over ice cream.

BETTER HOMES AND GARDENS BOOKS
NEW YORK • DES MOINES

© Meredith Corporation, 1970, 1971, 1973. All Rights Reserved.
Printed in the United States of America.
Special Edition. First Printing.
Library of Congress Catalog Card Number: 73-83173
SBN: 696-02024-6

CANNING

How to preserve fruits, vegetables, and meats
with instructions for each canning method.

Canning is a preservation method by which food is sealed in containers and is usually processed with heat. During the processing time, heat cooks the food and renders it safe for shelf storage at room temperature.

The principles of canning were first established by a Frenchman named Nicolas Appert. In 1809, he was awarded a prize by Napoleon for developing a food preservation method that eased the problem of providing food for the French Army. Appert's method involved heating food in sealed containers. At the time, Appert did not understand the true reason for food preservation. He believed the food did not spoil because it was sealed in an airtight container, when in fact it was the destruction of bacteria by heat that was responsible. This was explained by Louis Pasteur more than a half-century later.

In 1819, ten years after Appert chanced on his method for canning food, the development of commercial canning began in America. The development of home canning methods is credited to the more adventurous homemakers with their successful, yet crude efforts to preserve the excess food produced during the bountiful harvests. Later came the advanced home canning methods in use today.

The success of canning is dependent upon the destruction of microorganisms and/or enzymes which may cause spoilage. Commercially canned food which is heated to destroy these agents is termed commercially sterile. However, it is not possible always to destroy all microorganisms that are present. A few heat-resistant organisms can only be destroyed by heating to such high temperatures that the food in turn becomes undesirable. Fortunately, these types of organisms need not be destroyed since they are harmless.

Obviously the selection of high-quality food is of the utmost importance. Regardless of whether food is canned commercially or at home, the chance for spoilage is greater in food which has started to decay than in food which is of top quality.

Nutritional value: Canning does not significantly change the nutrient value of food. There is little difference in raw or canned food in caloric, protein, fat, or carbohydrate content. However, a slight-to-moderate loss of some of the less-stable vitamins does occur during processing, and other vitamins and minerals dissolve out of the food and into the liquid surrounding the food. This can be remedied easily by serving the canning liquid with the food. This liquid is often termed "the elixir of life."

How to store: Both commercially canned and home canned food are safe for shelf storage although a loss of quality may be noted over a prolonged period of time. If food is canned at home, always label the container with (1) date of canning, and (2) kind of food. By knowing this information, the food can be used accordingly to avoid excessively long periods of storage.

You might also like to make a note of any special information for later reference, such as type of seeds planted for home grown foods, recipe used, any recipe changes, or special seasonings added. Then, there won't be any guessing about how you canned the food so you can repeat or modify the procedure when canning again.

Regardless of whether food is canned commercially or at home, it is best stored in a dry place at a moderately cool temperature. Avoid storage near hot water pipes, radiators, or kitchen ranges. If glass jars are used, storage in the dark may help preserve the natural color of the food. Unless the seal of the container is broken, canned food will not spoil when frozen. However, a softening of texture usually results, making the food less desirable.

Some commercially canned foods, such as the larger canned hams, require special storage. These hams have been pasteurized but have not been canned by conventional methods. They should be refrigerated before opening. However, some of the smaller hams canned by conventional methods are shelf stable. It is necessary always to check the label on the container for special storage instructions.

After commercially canned *or* home canned food is opened, it should be refrigerated. Any unused portion of food may be stored safely in the open can, provided it is covered and placed in the refrigerator.

How to use: Home canned meats, poultry, fish, and vegetables (except tomatoes) must be heated at boiling temperature for 10 to 20 minutes before tasting or using. This is important since some forms of spoilage are not visible. By boiling, you will destroy any unknown spoilage agents.

Due to the more scientifically controlled conditions under which foods are canned commercially, they need not undergo the same precautionary period of cooking required for home canned foods. Commercially canned foods, unless labeled otherwise, can be eaten directly from the can without heating. The same is true of home canned fruits and tomatoes.

Commercial canning

Scientific advances in microbiology in addition to the development and refinement of equipment paved the way for the growth of the canning industry. As a result, food canned by commercial methods has met wide acceptance since it offers a convenient and safe means for preserving food.

Canned food is more easily transported than many fresh foods and does not require refrigeration necessary for fresh or frozen foods. Likewise, the storage of canned food in the home is often less costly than the storage of fresh or frozen food. Also, canning makes many seasonal foods available the year round. Thus, canned food often provides the homemaker with a wider selection of food at a lower cost.

Equipment: At first the containers used for canning were wide-mouthed glass bottles sealed with corks. Later experimentation with earthenware containers proved unsuccessful. In time, however, the more efficient and economic tin containers were accepted in the canning industry. The earliest tin cans were filled through small openings in the top. Later, open-topped containers, which could be sealed after filling, were developed for commercial use.

Today, containers made of steel plate coated with tin are used. Some foods, such as red fruits and certain vegetables, may discolor if they are canned in tin. Consequently, containers used in canning these foods are coated with a special enamel finish. In addition, glass containers with tight seals are sometimes used by commercial canners for canning food.

Methods of canning: The conventional method of commercial canning is similar to home canning methods. After the food is sealed in the container, it is heated (usually under pressure) for a certain length of time, depending upon the type of food. Then after processing, the containers are cooled quickly to stop the cooking.

While heating the food destroys bacteria, it does present certain problems to the canner. For example, since heat must travel from the outside of the container to the center, there is a tendency to overcook food near the edge of the container. To overcome this, new methods and equipment are continually being developed.

In one method, cans are agitated during processing in an attempt to speed up the distribution of heat throughout the food. Likewise, higher temperatures and shorter processing times are utilized.

Another method employs even higher temperatures and shorter processing times. After the food is sterilized, it is packed into sterilized containers under aseptic conditions. A variation of this method involves packing sterilized food into sterilized containers under pressure. A short processing is sometimes used after sealing.

Today, a wide selection of special dietetic foods, canned without the addition of salt, sugar, or with less fat, is available in the supermarket and specialty stores.

Home canning

Foods canned at home are popular with many families not only for economy, but also for a "fresh-from-your-garden" flavor possible for home canned fruits and vegetables. In addition to these foods, meats, poultry, jams, jellies, relishes, and pickles are often canned at home.

The three methods of canning recommended for home canning of food are (1) raw pack, (2) hot pack, and (3) open kettle. Food prepared by either the raw or hot pack method is then processed in a (1) pressure canner, (2) pressure saucepan, or (3) water bath canner. Food canned by the open kettle method is not processed since the food is thoroughly cooked before it is placed in the containers. A specific canning and processing method is often recommended for canning a particular food. (For best results, follow the canning and processing methods outlined below and in the accompanying charts.)

Equipment: Although you may purchase some equipment made especially for canning, many items may already be available in your kitchen. For example, brushes, knives, colanders, sieves, and scales are useful in canning. A large wire basket or similar utensil is convenient for blanching (dipping food into boiling water) fruits and vegetables. A funnel or ladle is handy for filling containers. In addition, large tongs are necessary for handling hot jars or cans after the processing.

For water bath canning, you need a big, tightly covered metal container. It should be deep enough for an inch or two of water over the tops of the jars plus a few inches for brisk boiling. A large rack placed in the bottom of the canner can be used for holding the jars. This prevents direct contact between the containers and the canner, and if the rack has handles, provides easy removal of hot jars.

A pressure canner is required for canning food under pressure. Check the pres-

---

Common container sizes

Check labels for exact net weights as different foods packed in identical containers vary in weight due to different densities.

Container size	Approximate net weight or fluid measure	Approximate Cups
8 ounce	8 ounces	1
Picnic	10½ to 12 ounces	1¼
12 ounce (vacuum)	12 ounces	1½
No. 300	14 to 16 ounces	1¾
No. 303	16 to 17 ounces	2
No. 2	20 ounces or 18 fluid ounces	2½
No. 2½	27 to 29 ounces	3½
No. 3 cylinder or 46 fluid ounce	51 ounces or 46 fluid ounces	5¾
No. 10	6½ pounds to 7 pounds 5 ounces	12 to 13

How to select: When purchasing canned food, avoid cans which bulge or cans in which there is evidence that the seal has been broken. A dented or rusted can is safe so long as the seal has not been broken.

Be certain to read carefully the label on the can. It not only states the brand name, but also the name of the food, the name of the manufacturer or distributor, and the net weight or volume of the contents. There may be an illustration, a description of the contents in terms of variety, the style of pack (water or syrup—light, heavy, or extra heavy), the amount of food in the can stated in cups or number of pieces, or suggested serving ideas and recipes.

The concern for special diets has not gone unnoticed by the canning industry.

sure gauge for accuracy and never attempt to use a pressure canner which is not working properly. If you process only a small amount of food and use small containers, a pressure saucepan may be substituted.

The selection of containers for canning is important. Use either glass jars, or cans made of steel plate coated with tin. Personal preference as well as the particular food to be canned will determine the final selection of containers that are used.

There are many advantages to using glass jars in home canning: although the initial expense of glass is greater than for cans, jars can be used and reused for many years; the sealing lid or rubber is the only part that must be replaced with each canning; less equipment is required for sealing glass jars than is needed for metal containers, and many homemakers prefer to use jars because the food can be seen after canning. The pride of many home canning enthusiasts is the attractive pack visible only in glass containers. Another advantage to choosing glass containers is that they may be used for canning all foods. This is particularly important when canning red fruits, pumpkin, rhubarb, winter squash, corn, and hominy as they may become discolored unless glass or enamel-coated metal containers are used.

But this is not to suggest metal cans do not have some advantages: cans, if not dented or damaged, can be used for more than one canning; since the sealing is done by a mechanical sealer before processing, there is no loss of liquid from cans regardless of fluctuation in pressure; a more rapid cooling after processing is possible with metal, and metal cans protect food from light thus preventing discoloration of the food during storage. These are distinct advantages over glass jar canning where the sealing does not occur until after processing, and where a rapid loss of pressure may cause loss of liquid or even breakage of the container during canning.

Different-sized containers—glass or metal—are available and should be selected according to the amount of food to be canned, the storage available, the size of family, and intended use of the food.

The two most common types of covers for glass jars are (1) a metal lid edged with a sealing compound which is secured to the jar with a metal screw band, and (2) a zinc porcelain-lined cover with a shoulder rubber ring. Either of these covers works satisfactorily; however, they should be checked before each use. Brittle or inelastic rubber rings and new metal sealing discs must be replaced before each canning. Since sealing compounds differ, always follow the lid manufacturer's directions for the correct method of use.

The sealing of metal cans is accomplished with a continuous ring of sealing compound which is found around the edge of the lid. When heated, the sealing compound melts and seals the container.

Methods of canning: The preliminary steps to canning involve preparing and packing the food into the containers. Three methods—raw pack, hot pack, and open kettle—may be used. However, each method is recommended only for certain foods. These recommendations are based upon safety and quality retention of the food.

Raw pack method—the uncooked food is packed into the containers and then a boiling liquid—syrup, water, or fruit juice—is added. Processing can be done either in a water bath or in a pressure cooker. The raw pack method is recommended for canning most fruits and tomatoes. Other vegetables may be canned raw pack *if they are processed in a pressure canner.*

Hot pack method—the food is partially cooked before it is packed into the containers. This method is used in canning vegetables, meats, and some fruits. Although most fruits may be canned either raw or hot pack, apples, applesauce, and rhubarb are recommended for hot pack.

Open kettle canning—the food is cooked (but not necessarily sterilized) before it is sealed in the containers and no further processing is required. This method of canning is recommended for jams, jellies, preserves, conserves, fruit butters, and other foods relatively high in sugar or acid.

Methods of processing: Processing is the correct application of heat to food packed in containers to render it safe for storage: over processing results in overcooked food that is still safe for storage, underprocessed food is unsafe. Processing can be done in a pressure canner or cooker, pressure saucepan, or water bath canner.

Pressure canner or cooker—this is necessary for low-acid foods such as meats and vegetables (except tomatoes, sauerkraut, and ripe pimiento peppers), since in low-acid foods some spoilage agents are not destroyed by boiling temperatures, and therefore, higher temperatures are necessary. This is possible only when a pressure canner or cooker is used.

To use a pressure canner, stand the containers on a rack in the bottom of the canner in two to three inches of water, leaving a small space between each container. Fasten the cover securely and allow the steam to escape steadily for ten minutes before closing the pet cock or vent.

The processing time begins when the pressure gauge reaches a specified pressure. Maintain the pressure at a constant point by adjusting the heat under the canner. Do not attempt to lower the pressure by opening the pet cock or vent as this will cause a loss of liquid from the jars. When the processing time is up, first remove the canner from the heat, then let the pressure drop gradually to zero before opening the pet cock or vent. Then open the cover and carefully remove the containers with tongs. Cool containers on a rack or cloth, a few inches apart, and away from drafts.

Altitude correction

For water bath canning, add 1 minute to processing time if time specified is 20 minutes or less, for each 1,000 feet above sea level. Add 2 minutes for every 1,000 feet if time called for is more than 20 minutes.

For pressure canning, increase pressure 1 pound for each 2,000 feet above sea level.

Pressure saucepan—this can be used for processing pints or other small containers. It must be equipped with a gauge for showing and maintaining a constant pressure of ten pounds. For processing times, add 20 minutes to the time recommended for processing in a pressure canner. Follow the manufacturer's instructions for detailed canning directions.

Water bath canner—this is used for processing high-acid foods such as fruits, tomatoes, sauerkraut, ripe pimiento peppers, and pickles. Place the containers in a large kettle and fill to one inch above the tops of the containers with water that is just below the boiling point. Arrange the containers so they are not touching, then cover the kettle. The processing time begins when the water comes to a full boil. Keep the water boiling gently. If necessary, add more boiling water to keep tops of containers covered. When time is up, remove the containers and place them on a rack or cloth, positioned a few inches apart, and away from all drafts.

Home canned fruits

Select fresh, firm fruits for canning. To insure even cooking, sort fruit according to size and ripeness. Thoroughly wash fruit under running water or through several changes of water; handle fruit gently to avoid bruising. Use ascorbic acid color keeper on apples, peaches, and pears to prevent the cut surfaces of the fruit from darkening during preparation. Most fruits may be canned either raw pack or hot pack. However, they are most often processed in a water bath canner. To can fruits, follow detailed directions below.

1. Check jars and lids for flaws. Discard any with chips or cracks. Use all new metal sealing discs or rubbers.

2. Wash jars in hot, sudsy water; rinse. Wash lids according to manufacturer's directions. Place jars in hot water till ready to use. They needn't be sterilized as this is done during the processing.

3. Place water bath canner on heat with enough water to cover tops of jars.

4. Prepare fruit according to chart (see page 395) using either the raw or hot pack method. Use a very light, light, medium, or heavy syrup to suit personal taste.

Raw pack: (May be used for all fruits except apples and applesauce.) Firmly pack fruit into jars. Leave ½-inch headspace at top of jar. Pour in boiling syrup, still leaving ½-inch headspace.

Hot pack: (May be used for all fruits.) Precook fruit in syrup according to chart. Loosely pack hot fruit into jars leaving ½-inch headspace (¼-inch headspace for applesauce). Cover fruit with boiling syrup, leaving the same amount of headspace.

5. Force out air bubbles from filled jars by working blade of table knife down sides of jars. Add more liquid if needed, but keep the original headspace.

6. Adjust jar caps: (a) For *two-piece metal lids*, wipe sealing edge of jar with clean cloth to remove food particles; put metal lid on jar with sealing compound next to glass. Screw band tight. (b) For *porcelain-lined zinc screw covers*, fit wet rubber ring on jar; wipe jar rim and ring with clean cloth. Partially seal by screwing the zinc cover down firmly, then turn the cover back ¼ inch.

7. Lower jars on rack into the water bath canner (have water just below the boiling point). Be sure jars do not touch. Cover the canner. The processing time begins when the water returns to a rolling boil. Boil gently during entire processing time. Add more *boiling* water as needed to keep jars covered. Process fruit according to the time indicated on chart. Note altitude corrections (see page 391).

8. After processing, remove hot jars from canner. Cool on rack or cloth, a few inches apart, and away from drafts for time specified by lid manufacturer.

To release air bubbles, work blade of table knife down side of filled jar. This insures all food is covered with liquid.

9. Check seals on jars when cold. To test jar with metal lid, press center of lid; if lid is drawn down, jar is sealed. For other types of covers, tip jar to check for leakage. If jar isn't sealed, use immediately; or, check jar for flaws and reprocess with a new lid following original procedure.

10. To store jars, remove screw bands from two-piece metal lids. Wipe jars; label with contents and date. Store in cool, dry, and dark place for up to one year.

When ready to use canned fruit, puncture metal disc and lift up. For zinc screw covers, pull out rubber ring, using pliers, before unscrewing cap. Look for spoilage —leaks, bulging lids, or off-odor. Never taste food with these signs; discard.

Home canned meats

Meat may be canned using the raw or hot pack method. Do not add liquid to meat if canned raw pack. Meat must be processed in a pressure canner. Follow instructions for canning meat as given below.

1. Check jars and lids for flaws. Discard any with chips or cracks. Use all new metal sealing discs or rubbers.

2. Wash jars in hot, sudsy water; rinse. Wash lids according to manufacturer's directions. Place jars in hot water till ready to use. They needn't be sterilized.

Canned fruit yield

Generally, for 1 quart canned fruit use the following amount of fresh fruit as purchased:

Fruit	Pounds
Apples	2½ to 3
Berries, except strawberries	1½ to 3
Cherries (if canned unpitted)	2 to 2½
Peaches	2 to 3
Pears	2 to 3
Plums	1½ to 2½

Canning fruit			
Fruit	**Preparation of Fruit** Very Light Syrup: 1cup sugar to 4 cups water = 4¾ cups Light Syrup: 2 cups sugar to 4 cups water = 5 cups Medium Syrup: 3 cups sugar to 4 cups water = 5½ cups Heavy Syrup: 4¾ cups sugar to 4 cups water = 6½ cups Boil sugar and water together 5 minutes. Skim if needed.	**Water bath in minutes (Pints)**	**Water bath in minutes (Quarts)**
Apples	*Hot Pack:* Wash, pare, core, and cut in pieces. While preparing, treat to prevent darkening with ascorbic acid color keeper following package directions for fresh-cut fruit. Boil in syrup or water 5 minutes. Pack hot; cover with boiling syrup or water leaving ½-inch headspace. Adjust lids; process in boiling water bath.	15	20
	Applesauce: Prepare sauce; heat to simmering; pack hot into hot jars leaving ¼-inch headspace. Adjust lids; process in boiling water bath.	10	10
Apricots Peaches Pears	*Raw Pack:* Wash and peel fruit (dip peaches and apricots in boiling water, then in cold water for easier peeling) *or* omit peeling apricots, if desired. Halve or slice; pit or core. While preparing, use ascorbic acid color keeper following package directions for fresh-cut fruit. Pack into hot jars; cover with boiling syrup leaving ½-inch headspace. Adjust lids; process in boiling water bath.	25	30
	Hot Pack: Prepare as above. Heat through in syrup. Pack hot into hot jars; cover with boiling syrup leaving ½-inch headspace. Adjust lids; process in boiling water bath.	20	25
Berries (except strawberries)	*Raw Pack:* Use for raspberries, other soft berries. Wash fruit; drain. Fill hot jars. Cover with boiling syrup leaving ½-inch headspace. Adjust lids; process in boiling water bath.	10	15
	Hot Pack: Use for firm berries. Wash; drain. Add ½ cup sugar to each quart berries. Bring to boil in covered pan; shake pan to keep berries from sticking. Pack hot into hot jars leaving ½-inch headspace. Adjust lids; process in boiling water bath.	10	15
Cherries	*Raw Pack:* Wash, stem, and pit, if desired. Fill hot jars. Cover with boiling syrup leaving ½-inch headspace. Adjust lids; process in boiling water bath.	20	25
	Hot Pack: Wash; remove pits, if desired. Add ½ cup sugar to each quart fruit. Add a little water only to *unpitted* cherries. Cover; bring to boiling. Pack hot into hot jars leaving ½-inch headspace. Adjust lids; process in boiling water bath.	10	15
Plums	*Raw Pack:* Wash; prick skins if canning whole fruit. Halve and pit freestone plums, if desired. Pack into hot jars. Cover with boiling syrup leaving ½-inch headspace. Adjust lids; process in boiling water bath.	20	25
	Hot Pack: Prepare as above. Bring to boil in syrup. Pack hot into hot jars; add boiling syrup leaving ½-inch headspace. Adjust lids; process in boiling water bath.	20	25
Rhubarb	Wash; cut into ½-inch pieces. Pack rhubarb into hot jars, leaving ½-inch headspace. Cover with boiling light syrup, leaving ½-inch headspace. Adjust lids; process in boiling water bath.	10	10
Fruit juices	Wash fruit; pit, if desired. Crush fruit; heat to simmering; strain through cheesecloth bag. Add sugar, if desired (1 cup per gallon of juice). Heat to simmering. Fill hot jars with hot juice leaving ½-inch headspace. Adjust lids; process in boiling water bath.	5	5

3. Clean and prepare meat or poultry according to chart (see below).

4. Pack meat into jars using either the raw or hot pack method.

Raw pack: Loosely pack raw meat in jars, leaving 1-inch headspace. Don't add liquid. There is less shrinkage of pre-cooked meats that are packed hot, but you may like the texture of the canned meats better if they are packed raw.

Hot pack: Cook meat or poultry in a small amount of water or broth till medium done. (If desired, remove bones from poultry.) Loosely pack cooked meat into jars, leaving 1-inch headspace. Cover with broth or boiling water, leaving 1-inch headspace. Force out air bubbles from filled jars by working blade of table knife down sides of jars. Add more liquid if needed, but keep original 1-inch headspace.

5. Add ½ teaspoon salt to each quart.

6. Adjust jar caps: (a) For *two-piece metal lids,* wipe jar rim with clean cloth to remove grease or food; put metal lid on jar with sealing compound next to glass. Screw band tight. (b) For *porcelain-lined zinc screw covers,* fit wet rubber ring on jar; wipe jar rim and ring with cloth. Partially seal by screwing zinc cap down firmly, then turn the cover back ¼ inch.

7. Place jars on rack in pressure canner containing two to three inches of hot water. Leave a small amount of space between the jars. Securely fasten cover. Let the steam escape steadily for ten minutes before closing the pet cock or vent. The processing time begins when the gauge reaches a specified pressure. Keep pressure constant. Process according to chart. Note altitude corrections (see page 391).

Canning meat			
Meat	Preparation of Meat	Pressure canner minutes at 10 lbs. (Pints)	Pressure canner minutes at 10 lbs. (Quarts)
	Chill meat immediately after slaughter. Pack meat loosely in jars leaving 1-inch headspace at top of jar. Add 1 teaspoon salt per quart, if desired.		
Beef Veal Lamb Pork Venison	Chill meat immediately after slaughter. Wipe the meat with a clean, damp cloth. Soak venison in salt water (¼ cup salt to 1 quart water) for 1 to 2 hours; drain. Cube the meat or cut meat into jar-length pieces so grain runs length of jar. Remove all gristle, bones, and as much fat as possible. *Raw Pack:* Pack loosely into hot jars, leaving 1-inch headspace. Add ½ teaspoon salt to each quart jar. Do not add liquid. Adjust lids. Process. *Hot Pack:* Simmer meat in a small amount of water in a covered pan till medium-done; stir occasionally. Season lightly with salt. *Or* brown the meat in small amount of fat. Season lightly with salt. Pack the meat loosely into hot jars, leaving 1-inch headspace. Fill with boiling water or broth, leaving 1-inch headspace. Adjust lids. Process in pressure canner.	75 75	90 90
Poultry Chicken Duck Turkey Game Birds Rabbit	Rinse chilled, dressed poultry in cold water. Soak rabbit in salt water (¼ cup salt to 1 quart water) 1 to 2 hours. Pat dry with clean cloth. Cut up meat. Remove visible fat. *Raw Pack:* Do not remove bones (except breastbone, if desired). Pack loosely into hot jars. (For poultry, place thigh and drumsticks with skin next to glass and fit breast pieces into center.) Leave 1-inch headspace. Add ½ teaspoon salt to each quart. Do not add liquid. Adjust lids. Process. *Hot Pack:* Boil, steam, or bake poultry just until meat can be removed from the bone. Take meat off the bones, if desired, but do not remove skin. Pack the meat pieces loosely into hot jars. (For poultry, place thigh and drumsticks with skin next to glass and fit breast pieces into the center.) Leave 1-inch headspace. Add ½ teaspoon salt to each quart. Cover with boiling water or broth, leaving 1-inch headspace. Adjust lids. Process in pressure canner.	boned 75 bone-in 65 boned 75 bone-in 65	90 75 90 75

8. When time is up, remove center from heat; let the pressure drop to zero. Then open the pet cock slowly; unfasten the cover. Remove jars. Cool on cloth or rack, a few inches apart, and away from drafts for the time specified by lid manufacturer.

9. Check seal on jars when cold. To test jar with metal lid, press center of lid; if lid is drawn down, the jar is sealed. For other types of caps, tip jar to check for leakage. If jar isn't sealed, use immediately; or, check jar for flaws and reprocess immediately with a new lid.

10. To store jars, remove screw band from two-piece metal lid. Wipe jars; label with contents and date. Store in cool, dry, and dark place for up to one year.

When ready to use canned meat or poultry, puncture metal disc and lift up. For zinc screw covers, pull out rubber ring, using pliers, before unscrewing cap. Look for spoilage—leaks, bulging lids, or off-odor. Never taste foods with these signs. Boil all meat 10 minutes before tasting.

Home canned vegetables

Most vegetables may be canned either raw or hot pack. The method used is a matter of personal preference. However, all vegetables (except tomatoes, sauerkraut, and ripe pimiento peppers) must be processed in a pressure canner for safety. Tomatoes and other high-acid vegetables are generally processed in a water bath canner.

Select fresh, firm vegetables for canning. Sort according to size to insure even cooking if vegetables are canned whole, such as beets, mushrooms, or new potatoes. Also, sort according to ripeness. Follow detailed instructions given below.

1. Check jars and lids for flaws. Discard any with chips or cracks. Use all new metal sealing discs or rubbers.

2. Wash jars in hot, sudsy water; rinse. Wash lids according to manufacturer's directions. Place jars in hot water till ready to use. They needn't be sterilized as this is done during processing

3. Wash and trim vegetables according to chart (see pages (396-397). For tomatoes, follow recipe directions (see page 398).

4. Pack vegetables into jars using either the raw or hot pack method.

Raw pack: Asparagus, lima beans, green beans, carrots, corn, and peas may be packed by this method. (Can cream-style corn in pint jars only.) Firmly pack raw vegetables into hot jars (except pack limas, corn, and peas loosely). Leave ½-inch headspace at top of jar (1 inch for lima beans, corn, potatoes, and peas). Pour boiling water into jars, leaving ½-inch headspace (1 inch for lima beans, corn, potatoes, and peas).

Hot pack: All vegetables may be packed by this method. Precook vegetables for time indicated on chart. Loosely pack boiling vegetables into hot jars; leave ½ inch headspace (1 inch for lima beans, corn, peas, and potatoes). Add boiling liquid; leave same headspace as above.

5. Force out air bubbles from filled jars by working blade of table knife down sides of jars. Add more liquid if needed, but keep the original headspace.

6. Add ½ teaspoon salt to each quart. (If desired, salt may be omitted.)

7. Adjust jar caps: (a) For *two-piece metal lids,* wipe jar rim with clean cloth to remove food particles; put metal lid on jar with sealing compound next to glass. Screw band tight. (b) For *porcelain-lined zinc screw covers,* fit wet rubber ring on jar; wipe jar rim and ring with clean cloth. Partially seal by screwing cap down firmly, then turn cap back ¼ inch.

8. Place jars on rack in pressure canner containing two to three inches hot water. Leave small amount of space between jars. Fasten cover securely. Let a steady flow of steam escape for two minutes before closing pet cock or vent. Processing time begins when the gauge reaches the specified pressure. Keep pressure constant. Process according to chart. Note altitude corrections (see page 391).

9. When time is up, remove canner from heat; let pressure drop to zero. Open pet cock or vent slowly; unfasten cover. Remove jars with tongs. Cool on rack or cloth, a few inches apart, and away from drafts for time specified by lid manufacturer.

10. Check seal on jars when cold. To test metal lid, press center of lid; if lid is drawn down, jar is sealed. For other caps, tip jars to check for leakage. If not sealed, use immediately; or, check for flaws and reprocess immediately with a new lid.

Canning vegetables			
Vegetable	Preparation of Vegetables Precook; pack into jar with hot cooking water to ½ inch from top unless otherwise specified. Add ½ teaspoon salt to each quart. Or, pack raw; cover with boiling water. Leave head-space as specified; add ½ teaspoon salt per quart.	Pressure canner minutes at 10 lbs. (Pints)	Pressure canner minutes at 10 lbs. (Quarts)
Asparagus	Wash; trim off scales and tough ends; cut in 1-inch pieces. *Hot Pack:* Cook in boiling water 3 minutes; pack hot. Add salt, boiling cooking liquid: leave ½-inch headspace. Adjust lids; process. *Raw Pack:* Pack tightly into jars; add salt; cover with boiling water. Leave ½-inch headspace; adjust lids; process.	25 25	30 30
Beans Green and Wax	Wash; trim ends; cut in 1-inch pieces. *Hot Pack:* Cook 5 minutes in boiling water. Pack hot; add salt, hot cooking liquid; leave ½-inch headspace. Adjust lids; process. *Raw Pack:* Pack in jars; add salt; cover with boiling water. Leave ½-inch headspace; adjust lids; process.	20 20	25 25
Beans Lima	*Hot Pack:* Shell and wash young beans; cover with boiling water; bring to boil. Pack loosely to 1 inch from top of jar. Add salt and boiling water; leave 1-inch headspace; adjust lids; process. *Raw Pack:* Shell and wash young beans; pack loosely to 1 inch from top of pint jar, 1 inch from top of quart jar. Add salt and boiling water; leave 1-inch headspace; adjust lids; process.	40 40	50 50
Beets	Wash, leaving on root and 1 inch of tops. Cover with boiling water; precook about 15 minutes. Slip off skins and trim; cube or slice large beets. Pack hot. Add salt and boiling water. Leave ½-inch headspace. Adjust lids; process.	30	35
Carrots	*Hot Pack:* Wash and pare; slice or dice. Cover with boiling water and bring to boil. Pack hot; add salt and boiling cooking liquid. Leave ½-inch headspace. Adjust lids; process. *Raw Pack:* Wash; pare; slice or dice. Pack tightly into jars; add salt, boiling water. Leave ½-inch headspace. Adjust lids, process.	25 25	30 30
Corn Whole kernel	Cut corn from cob; do not scrape cob. *Hot Pack:* Add 2 cups boiling water per 1 quart of corn; bring to boil. Pack hot corn loosely. Add salt and boiling hot cooking liquid leaving 1-inch headspace. Adjust lids; process. *Raw Pack:* Pack corn loosely to 1 inch from top. Add salt. Cover with boiling water leaving 1-inch headspace. Adjust lids; process.	55 55	85 85
Cream- style	Cut corn from cob, cutting only about half the kernel; scrape cob. *Hot Pack:* Follow directions above; pack hot corn in pints only. *Raw Pack:* Follow directions above except pack to 1 inch from top of *pint* jars. Fill with boiling water; leave 1-inch headspace.	85 95	
Greens, all kinds	Wash thoroughly; cut out tough stems and midribs. Steam in cheese-cloth bag till well wilted, 10 minutes. Pack hot greens loosely. Add ¼ teaspoon salt to pints and ½ teaspoon salt to quarts; cover with boiling water. Leave ½-inch headspace; adjust lids; process.	70	90
Mushrooms	Wash thoroughly; trim stems. Slice, or leave small mushrooms whole. Steam 4 minutes or heat gently, covered, without liquid 15 minutes. Pack hot in pint jars; add ¼ teaspoon salt per pint. For good color use ascorbic acid color keeper (follow label directions). Cover with boiling water. Leave ½-inch headspace; adjust lids; process.	30	
Peas Green	*Hot Pack:* Shell; wash. Cover with boiling water; bring to boil. Pack hot peas loosely to 1 inch from top of jar. Add salt and boiling water. Leave 1-inch headspace; adjust lids; process. *Raw Pack:* Shell and wash peas. Pack loosely to 1 inch from top of jar. Add salt; cover with boiling water leaving 1-inch headspace. Adjust lids; process.	40 40	40 40

Potatoes New White	Wash; precook 10 minutes; remove skins. Pack hot; add salt; cover with boiling water. Leave 1-inch headspace. Adjust lids; process.	30	40
Sweet	*Dry Pack:* Wash; precook in boiling water 20 to 30 minutes. Remove skins; cut up. Pack hot to 1 inch from top; press gently; add no liquid or salt. Leave 1-inch headspace. Adjust lids; process.	65	95
	Wet Pack: Wash; boil till skins slip off easily. Remove skins; cut potatoes in pieces. Pack hot to 1 inch from top. Add salt. Cover with boiling water leaving 1-inch headspace. Adjust lids; process.	55	90
Pumpkin Squash Winter	Wash; remove seeds; pare and cube. Barely cover with water; bring to boil. Pack hot. Add salt; cover with boiling cooking liquid. Leave ½-inch headspace; adjust lids; process.	55	90
	Sieved pumpkin or squash: Wash; remove seeds. Pare and cut up. Steam about 25 minutes or till tender. Put through food mill or strainer. Heat through, stirring to prevent sticking. Pack hot. Add no liquid or salt. Leave ½-inch headspace; adjust lids; process.	65	80

Check jars for nicks and cracks before washing. Replace self-sealing lids; follow manufacturer's directions for cleaning.

Before covering, wipe jar rim with clean, damp cloth. Place lid with sealing compound down, next to glass; screw band tightly.

Use funnel to fill jars. For cold pack, cover vegetable with boiling water; leave headspace for expansion during processing.

11. To store jars, remove screw bands from two-piece metal lids. Wipe jars; label with contents and date. Store in a cool, dry, and dark place for up to one year.

To use vegetables, puncture metal disc and lift up. For zinc screw caps, pull out rubber ring, using pliers, before unscrewing the cap. Look for spoilage—leaks, bulging lids, spurting, or off odors. Never taste food with these signs. Even though spoilage may not be apparent, always boil corn and spinach 20 minutes before eating, and all other vegetables (except tomatoes) 10 minutes. Destroy food if an off-odor or foaming develops. (See *Jam, Jelly, Pickle* for additional information.)

To process meat or vegetables in pressure canner, arrange filled jars (not touching) in wire rack before placing in canner.

Lower jars on rack into canner containing 2 to 3 inches hot water. Follow manufacturer's directions for operating canner.

Stand jars apart and away from drafts to cool. To test seal, press down on center of lid. If lid is drawn down, jar is sealed.

Canning Tomatoes

Dip tomatoes in boiling water ½ minute; dip quickly in cold water. Remove stem ends; peel.

For raw pack: Pack tomatoes in jars; press gently to fill spaces. Leave ½-inch headspace. Add no water. Add ½ teaspoon salt to quarts. Adjust lids. Process in boiling water bath (see page 395, step 7), 35 minutes for pints or 45 minutes for quarts.

For hot pack: Quarter peeled tomatoes. Bring to boiling; stir constantly. Pack hot tomatoes into hot jars leaving ½-inch headspace. Add ½ teaspoon salt to quarts. Adjust lids. Process in boiling water bath (see page 392, step 7), 10 minutes for both pints and quarts.

For juice: Wash, remove stem ends, and cut tomatoes in pieces. Simmer until soft; stir often. Sieve. Add ½ teaspoon salt to each quart. Bring to boiling. Fill hot jars with hot juice leaving ½-inch headspace. Adjust lids. Process in boiling water bath (see page 392, step 7), 10 minutes for both pints and quarts.

Canned vegetable yield

Generally, for 1 quart canned vegetables prepare the following amount of fresh vegetable as picked or purchased:

Vegetable	Pounds
Asparagus	2½ to 4½
Beans, lima in pods	3 to 5
Beans, snap green	1½ to 2½
Beets, without tops	2 to 3½
Carrots, without tops	2 to 3
Corn, sweet in husks	3 to 6
Peas, green, in pods	3 to 6
Squash, winter	1½ to 3
Sweet potatoes	2 to 3
Tomatoes	2½ to 3½

CANTALOUPE, CANTALOUP, CANTALOPE, CANTELOPE—A member of the muskmelon family having a hard rind and a deep, apricot-colored flesh. Technically, the term cantaloupe should refer only to the hard rind variety of muskmelon. However, common usage has adopted the name to refer to the more popular netted variety.

Cantaloupe was named for the Castle of Cantalup, the home of a sixteenth century pope. It was in the Castle gardens that a variety of muskmelon brought from Armenia was first cultivated in Europe.

Cantaloupe was planted in the United States as early as 1609. However, no attempt was made to cultivate it commercially until near the close of the nineteenth century. Today, cantaloupe is produced commercially in 25 states with California being the leading producer.

Nutritional value: One-fourth of a five-inch cantaloupe supplies 30 calories while providing over two-thirds the daily adult requirement for vitamin A, and slightly less than half the daily requirement for vitamin C. Although other vitamins and minerals are present, they appear in much smaller amounts.

How to select: Cantaloupe is available throughout the year, but the largest supply appears on the market during the summer. Although a foolproof method for selecting a sweet, ripe, and juicy melon is

Captivate a summer luncheon with Cantaloupe Stars. To make bold zigzag edge, use a pencil to mark lines before cutting.

Uniformly shaped cantaloupe balls are simple to make with a melon-ball cutter. Serve alone or combine with other fresh fruits.

lacking, a few guides can be used as a fairly reliable indicator of quality.

A smooth calloused scar should be visible on the blossom end indicating the melon was mature when harvested, the netting should cover the melon thickly and stand out in bold relief, and it should have a dry, grayish color with the skin beneath the netting having a yellow tinge —too deep a yellow may indicate over-ripeness. Shape is another sign of quality; the rounder the melon, the sweeter the fruit. In addition, these are two other indications of maturity: there should be a delicate aroma at the blossom end, and a rattling of seeds in the melon when it is shaken.

How to store: If possible, plan to purchase melons a few days before using. Then, hold at room temperature two to three days. This allows the meat to soften and become juicy. However, if melons are ripe when purchased, they are best refrigerated to prevent over-ripening. Wash and dry melons. Wrap in moisture-vaporproof wrap, as the aroma of cantaloupe quickly penetrates other foods in the refrigerator.

How to use: A cantaloupe may be served in halves, wedges, slices, or balls. After cutting, remove all seeds and discard. The rind may or may not be removed.

Juicy melon balls peek from a fluffy lime filling in Seafoam Cantaloupe Pie. Top with whipped cream and sprinkle with toasted coconut for a cool and refreshing summertime dessert.

Served alone in the shell, cantaloupe makes an attractive breakfast fruit. Cut into balls, it is a refreshing addition to a fruit cup or salad. Cantaloupe à la mode features ice cream served in the hollow of the melon. (See also *Melon*.)

Tuna–Melon Dinner Salad

Combine 4 cups torn lettuce (½ large head); 2 cups cubed cantaloupe; one 11-ounce can mandarin oranges, drained; one 6½- or 7-ounce can tuna, drained and flaked; ¾ cup sliced process American cheese cut in strips; ½ cup chopped celery; ¼ cup sliced green onion; and ¼ cup sliced pitted ripe olives. Blend ½ cup mayonnaise and 1 tablespoon lemon juice; add to tuna mixture; toss. Makes 8 servings.

Cantaloupe Mist

Serve as a chilled, appetizer soup—

 1 **large ripe cantaloupe**
 ¼ **teaspoon ground cinnamon**
 1 **6-ounce can frozen orange juice**
   concentrate, thawed
 2 **juice cans water**
 2 **tablespoons lime juice**
   Lime wedges *or* mint sprigs

Halve melon; remove seeds and discard. Scoop out pulp. In blender container, combine melon pulp and cinnamon. Blend till puréed. Mix orange juice concentrate, water, and lime juice. Add melon purée. Chill. Serve in individual ice jackets; garnish each serving with lime wedge or mint sprig. Makes 6 cups.

Seafoam Cantaloupe Pie

> 1 envelope unflavored gelatin
>   (1 tablespoon)
> ½ cup sugar
> ¼ teaspoon salt
> 4 slightly beaten egg yolks
> ½ cup lime juice
> 1 teaspoon grated lime peel
>   Few drops green food coloring
> 4 egg whites
> ½ cup sugar
> ½ cup whipping cream
> 1½ cups cantaloupe balls
> 1 *baked* 9-inch pastry shell,
>   cooled (*See Pastry*)

Combine first 3 ingredients. Blend egg yolks, lime juice, and ¼ cup water; add to gelatin mixture. Cook and stir over medium heat just till mixture comes to boiling. Remove from heat; add lime peel and food coloring. Chill, stirring occasionally, till mixture mounds.

Beat egg whites to soft peaks; gradually add ½ cup sugar. Beat to stiff peaks. Fold in gelatin mixture. Whip cream; fold in whipped cream and cantaloupe. Pile into cooled pastry shell. Chill till firm. Top with additional whipped cream and toasted coconut, if desired.

Cantaloupe Stars

Stand a large cantaloupe on end. To cut zigzag edge, push sharp knife into center at an angle; pull out and make next cut at opposite angle (see picture, page 399). Repeat around melon. Pull halves apart; remove seeds.

Fill centers with a mixture of fresh fruits—strawberries, raspberries, pitted cherries or grapes, melon balls, or pineapple chunks. Drizzle thawed frozen lemonade concentrate over fruit. Chill. Makes 2 servings.

CANTONESE-STYLE COOKERY—A method of food preparation adapted from the cuisine of Canton, China and the surrounding area. (See also *Oriental Cookery*.)

CANVASBACK DUCK—A wild bird of North America prized for its flavor when roasted. It is named for the grayish, canvaslike appearance on its back. (See also *Duck*.)

CAPER—The flavor bud of the caper bush which is used to season or garnish food. Sometimes called "mountain pepper," the caper plant grows wild—mostly in dry, rocky places, from the Mediterranean to India. Bearing somewhat large, but short-lived white blossoms with purplish-stalked stamens, it is cultivated in the United States only for its decorative value.

The French variety of capers is considered superior to all others, including the English caper. The best capers are perfectly round, very small, and quite firm. Their flavor is pungent and slightly bitter. However, they should not be confused with pickled nasturtium seeds which are larger than caper buds, yet sometimes served as a substitute for capers.

Capers are most often pickled in vinegar and bottled, although sometimes they are available packed in salt. They are used frequently in the cuisine of many European as well as Southeast Asian countries. In the United States, imported pickled capers are most often used to garnish or add a flavor accent to hot and cold sauces, vegetables, salads, and meat dishes.

Caper Burgers

> ¼ cup butter or margarine
> 1 tablespoon drained capers
>   • • •
> 1½ pounds ground beef
> 1 teaspoon salt
>   Dash pepper
>   Kitchen bouquet
> 4 thick slices French bread,
>   toasted and buttered

Blend butter with capers. Form into 4 patties, ½ inch thick; turn out on waxed paper. Freeze till firm. Combine beef, salt, and pepper; shape into four 2-inch-thick oval patties, the size of French bread slices. Make depression in center of each, pressing down to ½ inch from bottom. Place frozen caper-butter patty in each depression. Mold meat to cover butter.

Brush with kitchen bouquet. Broil over *medium-hot* coals for 10 minutes. Turn carefully (so butter doesn't leak out) and broil 10 minutes more. Beef will be rare next to butter. Serve on toasted French bread. Makes 4 servings.

Jacques' Chicken Salad

    1 10-ounce package frozen
       French-style green beans,
       cooked and drained, *or* 1
       16-ounce can green beans, drained
    ¼ cup Italian salad dressing
    3 large chicken breasts, cooked,
       boned, and chilled
    ¼ cup whipping cream
    ½ cup mayonnaise
    1 cup diced celery
    3 lettuce cups
       Mayonnaise or salad dressing
    2 teaspoons drained capers
    6 tomato slices
    6 ripe olives
    2 hard-cooked eggs, quartered

Combine beans and Italian dressing. Chill several hours; stir occasionally. Cut 3 thin slices from chicken breasts and reserve. Cube remaining chicken. Whip cream. Gently fold the ½ cup mayonnaise into whipped cream.

Fold cubed chicken, celery, ½ teaspoon salt, and dash pepper into mayonnaise mixture. Chill thoroughly. Place lettuce cups on serving platter. Fill with chicken mixture. Top with reserved chicken slices and dollop of mayonnaise; sprinkle with capers. Drain beans; arrange between salads. Garnish with tomato slices, olives, and egg wedges. Makes 3 servings.

Caper Mayonnaise

Combine 1 cup mayonnaise or salad dressing; ¼ cup drained capers, coarsely chopped; 3 tablespoons chopped onion; and 2 tablespoons chopped toasted almonds. Serve warm or chilled over fish or vegetables. Makes 1½ cups.

CAPON (*kā' pon, -puhn*)—A rooster which has been castrated. When marketed, capons weigh from four to seven pounds. They provide a generous amount of white meat and fine flavor when roasted. (See also *Chicken*.)

An elegant salad for a special luncheon—Jacques' Chicken Salad. Capers dot chicken-capped salad served with marinated green beans, tomato slices, olives, and hard-cooked eggs.

Breast of Capon Isabelle

> 6 breasts of capon, boned,
>   skinned, and split lengthwise
> 2 tablespoons butter or margarine
> 2½ cups chicken stock
>   • • •
> 1 pound fine noodles
> 2 tablespoons butter or margarine
>   • • •
> 1 pint fresh mushrooms, sliced
>   (about 2 cups sliced)
> ¼ cup butter or margarine
> ¼ cup dry white wine
> ½ teaspoon salt
>   Dash pepper
> 2 tablespoons all-purpose flour
>   • • •
> ¼ cup butter or margarine
> ¼ cup all-purpose flour
> 1 teaspoon salt
> 2 cups light cream
> 3 slightly beaten egg yolks

In large skillet brown breasts in 2 tablespoons butter. Add *2 tablespoons* of the chicken stock. Cover; cook 30 minutes or till tender.

Meanwhile, cook noodles in boiling, salted water till tender; drain. Toss lightly with 2 tablespoons butter; keep hot.

Cook mushrooms in ¼ cup butter with wine, ½ teaspoon salt, and dash pepper till tender, about 5 minutes. Sprinkle with 2 tablespoons flour; stir to blend. Keep warm.

Remove breasts from skillet; keep warm. In same skillet, melt ¼ cup butter; blend in ¼ cup flour, 1 teaspoon salt, and dash pepper. Add remaining chicken stock and cream all at once. Cook and stir till mixture thickens and bubbles. Remove from heat; stir a little hot mixture into egg yolks. Return to hot mixture. Continue cooking, stirring constantly, just till mixture boils. Remove from heat.

Serve capon breasts on hot buttered noodles; top with mushroom mixture. Pour cream sauce over all. Makes 8 to 12 servings.

CAPPUCCINO (*kap' ŏŏ chē' nō, kä pŏŏ-*)— An Italian beverage prepared with espresso coffee and milk or whipping cream and served hot. Often it is served with a sprinkling of cinnamon and a cinnamon stick stirrer. (See also *Beverage*.)

Rich, dark espresso topped with whipped cream becomes an Italian favorite—Cappuccino. Serve with cinnamon stick stirrers.

Cappuccino

> ¼ cup instant espresso coffee
>   *or* instant coffee powder
> ½ cup whipping cream, whipped
>   Ground cinnamon *or* ground
>   nutmeg
>   Cinnamon stick stirrers

Dissolve coffee in 2 cups boiling water; pour into cups. Top each cup with spoonful of whipped cream; dash with cinnamon *or* nutmeg. Serve with cinnamon stick stirrers. Pass sugar, if desired. Makes 6 or 7 small servings.

CAPSICUM (*kap' suh kuhm*)—Any one of a number of pod-bearing plants native to tropical America. The many-seeded peppers borne by the numerous Capsicum varieties vary in size, color, and shape.

The Capsicum family may be divided into two classes—sweet and hot. Among the sweet is the bell or green pepper, most often used fresh. The hot varieties range from mildly warm to extremely hot, and include pimientos, chilies, and bird peppers. Sometimes used fresh, hot peppers most often are dried in the preparation of various seasonings such as chili powder, red pepper, cayenne, and paprika.

CAQUELON—A French earthenware casserole traditionally used for cheese fondue.

CARAMEL (*kar' uh muhl*)—1. A syrup made by cooking granulated sugar until it melts and changes color. 2. A rich chewy candy.

Caramel, the golden brown syrup, is used to flavor desserts, stews, and gravies. It is also known as burnt sugar.

Caramel candies are made with milk, butter and sugar. They are cut into cubes for serving. Commercial caramels come in butterscotch or chocolate flavors and in individual wraps. These caramels are used as candy or as an ingredient when melted with a liquid. (See also *Candy*.)

Caramels

    1 cup butter or margarine
    1 pound brown sugar (2¼ cups)
    1 cup light corn syrup
    1 15-ounce can sweetened
        condensed milk
    1 teaspoon vanilla

Melt butter or margarine in heavy 3-quart saucepan. Add sugar and dash salt; stir thoroughly. Stir in corn syrup; mix well. Gradually add milk, stirring constantly. Cook and stir over medium heat to firm-ball stage (245°), 12 to 15 minutes. Remove from heat; stir in vanilla. Pour into buttered 9x9x2-inch pan. Cool and cut candy into squares.

Caramel Cakewiches

    1 2-ounce package dessert
        topping mix
    1 large banana, sliced
    ½ 14-ounce package vanilla
        caramels (about 1½ cups)
    1 6-ounce can evaporated milk
        (⅔ cup)
    3 to 4 drops bitters
    6 slices pound cake

Prepare dessert topping mix according to package directions; fold in the sliced banana. Chill. In medium saucepan combine caramels and evaporated milk. Cook and stir over medium heat till caramels are melted; stir in bitters. To serve, top pound cake slices with banana mixture, then pour the warm caramel sauce over cakewich. Makes 6 servings.

CARAMELIZE—To change into caramel. Caramelizing is the process (1) of cooking granulated sugar until it melts, (2) of coating food with caramel, (3) of coating food with sugar and then cooking, or (4) of coating a mold or baking dish with caramel before adding the batter or food.

CARAWAY—An aromatic herb of the parsley family which has a tangy, pungent flavor. The caraway plant reaches the height of two feet and has green, feathery leaves and white flowers. The brown seeds are small (about three-sixteenths of an inch in length), curved, and tapered.

Caraway is an ancient herb. It was originally grown in the Caria region of Asia Minor from which the name caraway is derived. Roman soldiers brought the herb from Asia 2,000 years ago, thus helping it spread over all of their known world.

Caraway soon became popular as both a seasoning and a medicine. It developed as a distinctive part of German, English, Austrian, and Hungarian cookery. Used early as a medicine, it was credited with such feats as curing hysteria and restoring hair to the bald. Today, its value in medicines is still recognized.

The majority of caraway sold is imported from the Netherlands. However, it is cultivated in various parts of the United States, primarily in Maine. Whole caraway seed is the most common form of the herb found in the market and used for seasoning. These seeds can be stored for many years and not lose their aroma.

The entire caraway plant can be used for food. The fleshy root is cooked and eaten as a vegetable. The leaves, milder flavored than the seeds, are used to season soups, vegetables, and pork. Oil extracted from the seeds is a principle ingredient in the liqueur "kümmel."

You can use caraway seed as a seasoning in sauerkraut, coleslaw, stew, pork, bread, cookies, cheese, and vegetables. Rye bread's particular flavor comes from caraway. Caraway also gives a flavor-lift to carrots, spinach, or potato salad. Caraway is good combined with apple and can be used in many apple dishes. Also, caraway seed is good to munch after dinner, an ancient custom. (See also *Herb*.)

Austrian Cabbage Salad

    1 small head cabbage, shredded
        (6 cups)
    2 tablespoons salad oil
    2 tablespoons white wine vinegar
    2 tablespoons chopped green onion
    ½ teaspoon caraway seed
    ¼ teaspoon dried marjoram
        leaves, crushed
    ½ teaspoon salt
        Dash pepper
            • • •
    2 tablespoons snipped parsley
    1 tomato

Place cabbage in bowl; cover with boiling water. Let stand 5 minutes; drain well. To the cabbage add oil, vinegar, onion, caraway seed, marjoram, salt, and pepper. Toss; chill thoroughly. Just before serving, sprinkle salad with parsley. Cut tomato in wedges and place atop salad. Makes 6 servings.

Caraway Cookies

    1 cup butter or margarine
    1 cup sugar
    2 beaten eggs
  2¾ cups sifted all-purpose flour
    1 teaspoon baking soda
    ½ teaspoon cream of tartar
        Dash salt
    ½ cup chopped mixed candied
        fruits and peels
    ½ cup light raisins
    2 tablespoons caraway seed
    2 tablespoons rose water *or* water

Cream butter, sugar, and eggs till fluffy. Sift together flour, soda, cream of tartar, and salt; add to creamed mixture. Stir in candied fruits and peels, raisins, caraway seed, and water. Drop from teaspoon onto ungreased cookie sheet. Flatten with glass dipped in flour; center each with a light raisin. Bake at 375° for 8 to 10 minutes. Cool on rack. Makes 4½ dozen.

Caraway seed lends a pungent flavor and nutlike texture to cabbage. Try it in slaw, such as Austrian Cabbage Salad.

Caraway Fingers

6 frankfurter rolls
¼ cup garlic spread
¼ cup butter or margarine
¼ cup grated Parmesan cheese
2 teaspoons caraway seed

Quarter rolls lengthwise. Melt garlic spread and butter; brush on cut sides of rolls. Sprinkle with cheese, then caraway seed. Bake on cookie sheet at 450° for 5 to 8 minutes.

Caraway Chicken Halves

½ cup salad oil
¼ cup light corn syrup
¼ cup chopped onion
1 tablespoon lemon juice
1 teaspoon dried oregano leaves, crushed
1 teaspoon caraway seed
2 2- to 2½-pound ready-to-cook broiler-fryer chickens, halved lengthwise

Combine first 6 ingredients and ½ teaspoon salt. Brush over chicken halves. Place chicken halves on grill, bone side down. Broil over *slow* coals 25 minutes; turn, broil 20 minutes, brushing occasionally with herb mixture. Continue broiling, till meat is tender, about 10 minutes, turning occasionally and brushing with herb mixture. Makes 4 servings.

Caraway, identified by the feathery leaves and white flowers, is an attractive and useful herb to include in a home garden.

CARBOHYDRATE—A class of foods including sugars, starches, and cellulose. Sugars and starches provide energy for growth, maintenance, and activities of the body. Cellulose adds bulk to the diet.

Natural sources of carbohydrates are fruits, vegetables, milk, and cereals. Sugar is found in fruits, milk, and many vegetables. Rice, corn, potatoes, and wheat have a high starch content. Only a few foods, such as cane and beet sugar and cornstarch, are entirely made of carbohydrates. Some of these foods or foods made with them, such as bread and ice cream, should be eaten each day.

CARBONATED BEVERAGE—A drink which bubbles or fizzes because it has been charged with carbon dioxide under pressure. Many of these beverages are flavored with syrups, cola, and aromatic root.

Carbonated beverages are used as an ingredient with other foods as well as for chilled drinks served alone. They add sparkle and flavor to many gelatin salads, fruit punches, ice cream sodas, fruit sauces, dips, and desserts. They are also good as mixers for alcoholic beverages.

Once a container has been opened it should be tightly covered to keep the carbon dioxide from escaping for this causes a flat taste. (See also *Beverage.*)

Golden Glow Punch

1 3-ounce package orange-flavored gelatin
1 6-ounce can frozen pineapple-orange juice concentrate
4 cups apple juice
1 28-ounce bottle ginger ale, chilled (3½ cups)

Dissolve gelatin in 1 cup *boiling* water. Stir in pineapple-orange concentrate. Add apple juice and 3 cups cold water. Carefully pour in chilled ginger ale. Makes about 25 four-ounce servings of Golden Glow Punch.

CARBON DIOXIDE—A colorless, odorless gas. Carbon dioxide performs many functions in cooking. Baked foods are leavened

Pour carbonated beverages carefully down the *side* of glass just before serving to save those bubbles which give sparkle and zing.

by the carbon dioxide bubbles which are produced during the reaction of baking soda or baking powder and an acid. Carbon dioxide is also formed during fermentation and makes bubbles in beer and some wine. Carbonated beverages are bubbly because of this gas. Dry ice, its solid form, is often used to preserve foods.

CARDAMOM, CARDAMON *(kar' duh muhm)*

—A spice which tastes similar to anise and is sweeter than ginger. Its odor is pungent and sweet. Cardamom pods are the fruit of a plant of the ginger family. Each pod contains 17 to 20 tiny, black seeds.

This spice has been used for centuries in Indian and Scandinavian cookery. It may seem strange that two such distant countries share a love for the same spice. But the explanation is simple: cardamom is native to India and was discovered there by Vikings who took it to their countries 1,000 years ago. Cardamom is a traditional flavor in typical Indian dishes, such as curry, and in typical Danish pastries.

Cardamom is recognized as the world's second most precious spice. (Saffron is first.) It's expensive to produce since an acre yields only 250 pounds of the pods and each pod must be snipped from the plant by hand with scissors.

Whole pods, whole seeds, and ground cardamom are available. When recipes call for crushed cardamom, either the whole pod or whole seed can be used. Remove the outer soft shell if using pods; grind the seed to a powder with a mortar and pestle or crush with two tablespoons.

Cardamom awakens and accents the flavor of main dishes, orange slices, melons, jellies, fruit salads, and pastries, especially Christmas pastries. When flavoring with the spice, use the exact amount called for in the recipe, or add sparingly since it is quite pungent. (See also *Spice*.)

Cardamom Cookies

    1 cup sifted all-purpose flour
    ½ cup granulated sugar
    ⅛ or ¼ teaspoon ground cardamom
      Dash ground cinnamon
    ¼ teaspoon shredded lemon peel
    ¼ cup ground almonds
    6 tablespoons butter or margarine
    1 beaten egg
    2 teaspoons milk
      Granulated sugar

Sift together flour, sugar, cardamom, and cinnamon; stir in peel and almonds. Cut in butter till mixture resembles coarse crumbs. Stir in egg and milk till mixture forms a ball; chill.

Roll out to about ⅛-inch thickness. Cut into circles 1¾ inches in diameter. Place on ungreased cookie sheet; sprinkle with sugar. Bake at 400° till edges are brown, about 6 to 8 minutes. Makes about 7 dozen.

Crush whole cardamom seeds by removing the outer soft shell, placing in a tablespoon, and crushing with back of a second spoon.

CARDOON *(kär dōōn')*—A silvery green, thistlelike plant. Although it's related to the globe artichoke, cardoon looks more like celery. The flavor of cardoon is similar to both celery and artichoke.

Cardoon leaves and stalk are a popular vegetable in Europe, especially in the Mediterranean regions. To prepare it, cut into short pieces, boil in salted water till tender-crisp, and then chill. Eat with dressing, use in salads or soups, serve hot in a sauce with veal, or coat in batter and fry. (See also *Vegetable*.)

CARIBOU *(kar' uh bōō)*—A large North American deer related to reindeer of Europe and Asia. (See also *Game*.)

CAROTENE *(kar' uh tēn')*—Yellow and orange pigments in plants that the body converts into vitamin A when eaten.

Carotene is found in fruits and vegetables that are bright yellow and dark green. (The green color is due to chlorophyll which dominates the color of yellow carotene.) Rich sources are carrots, sweet potatoes, green pepper, and spinach.

An exception to the rule that carotene-rich foods are either yellow or dark green is some red foods. For example, watermelon, tomato, pink grapefruit, apricot, and persimmons are rich in carotene.

A few animal foods are natural sources of carotene or have carotene added. Milk, egg yolk, and butter have this pigment which gives them a yellow color. Sometimes the pigment is extracted from vegetables and added to butter or cheese for additional color as well as nutrition.

Each day adults and teen-agers need 5,000 International Units of vitamin A, either the vitamin itself or carotene which will be converted into the vitamin. Small children need about half this amount.

Carotene is necessary for normal growth and good eyesight. When converted to vitamin A, it keeps the skin, the lining of the respiratory and digestive tracts, and the surface of the eyes in a healthy condition. Certain symptoms indicate a deficiency of carotene. These are eye diseases, night blindness, low resistance to infection, slow growth, poor tooth enamel, and loss of reproductive power. However, an excessive intake over a long period of time causes carotenemia, a harmless condition with the spectacular effect of giving the skin a somewhat yellowish hue.

Carotene is quite stable. It's not soluble in water, nor is it destroyed by acid, alkali, or heat. Therefore, carotene is seldom lost during the process of cooking a food. (See also *Vitamin*.)

CARP—A large, freshwater fish. They are a gold to olive color, about two feet long, and can weigh as much as 40 pounds. Carp are hardy. They adapt to new locations easily, survive in waters unsuited for other fish, and live 20 to 40 years.

The carp is an immigrant. It moved from China to Europe, and then in 1876, it was brought to America from Germany.

Carp provides food and sport to some fishermen. Its roe can be made into a pseudo-caviar. Properly prepared, the firm, lean flesh is a flavorful food. Fillets or whole fish, ranging from two to seven pounds, are baked, broiled, fried, or stewed. They are good prepared in beer.

The better quality carp are caught in cold water. Therefore, November to April are the best months to buy or to catch and use fresh carp for food. Those available during the summer months may have a slightly muddy flavor. (See also *Fish*.)

CARRAGEEN *(kar' uh gēn)*—An edible seaweed, also called Irish moss. Carrageen is stubby and dark purple in color. It grows along the coast of Ireland.

Eat carregeen in the dried form or use it to thicken foods, such as pudding.

CARROT—A long, tapering, yellowish root. Both the root and feathery leaves of this vegetable are edible. As a member of the parsley family, it's related to dill, parsnip, Queen Ann's Lace, and deadly hemlock.

It was first grown, as history records, in Afghanistan and adjacent regions. Chinese, Japanese, and Indians are known to have used it for food in the thirteenth century. As the carrot spread into Europe, the people not only enjoyed it as a vegetable, but also found some additional uses. For instance, the Germans finely chopped and browned carrots for a coffee substitute. Then when the vegetable was introduced from Holland, English women adorned their hair with its feathery leaves.

Finally, in 1609, carrots were brought to the Americas. Virginia was the first colony known to have grown them, but soon other colonies and the American Indians were also cultivating this crop. Today, California, Texas, Michigan, Arizona, and Florida are the major areas where carrots are grown in the United States.

Nutritional value: Carrots are rich in carotene as the name suggests. When eaten, carotene is converted into vitamin A by the body. An average raw carrot or one-third cup of cooked carrots gives the day's requirement of vitamin A. Each raw carrot supplies about 21 calories.

Eating raw carrots is excellent for dental health. Chewing on this crisp vegetable exercises the teeth, gums, and jaw muscles and helps to clean the teeth.

How to select: The most abundant selection of fresh carrots is available during the months of January to June. However, fresh, frozen, and canned carrots are usually plentiful throughout the year.

Select fresh carrots that are firm, well-shaped, smooth, clean, and dark in color. Carrots which are shriveled or soft lack flavor. Large, chubby carrots with cracks are likely to be overgrown and fibrous. The darker the color, the more carotene it contains, so choose the brightest yellow and golden ones available. If you buy carrots with tops still on, be certain the leaves appear fresh and bright green.

Select young, small carrots which are more tender and milder flavored for eating raw. Older, larger ones are suitable for cooking and for shredding.

Fresh carrots are sold with or without tops in bundles and in plastic bags. Packages vary in weight, but figure a one pound package to make three servings.

Frozen and canned carrots are available in many forms. The consumer can choose diced, sliced, shoestring, or whole carrots. Frozen carrots with a brown sugar glaze or a butter sauce and carrot juice are additional selections which can be found in most grocery stores and supermarkets.

How to store: Fresh carrots will keep from one to four weeks when stored correctly. Remove any tops which are still attached to carrots as soon as possible. The tops reduce the quality of the carrot if left on, for they draw out moisture and nutrients. Before putting away, rinse the carrots and cover with foil, waxed paper, clean plastic wrap, or a plastic bag. Store in a cool, moist place. The crisper of the refrigerator or a cool basement, where air circulates, are good locations for storage.

Freeze or can fresh carrots for longer storage. Blanch, package, and freeze carrots; use within a year. (See *Canning* for additional ways to preserve carrots).

How to prepare: Remove skin from the carrots by thinly scraping with a vegetable peeler. If desired, scrub young carrots with a stiff brush to remove the skin.

To cook the carrots, leave whole, dice, slice, or shred. Place in a saucepan which contains 1 inch of boiling, salted water. Cover the saucepan and cook till tender. Shredded carrots will take about 5 minutes, small pieces about 10 to 20, and whole carrots about 15 to 20. Season the carrots, add butter or margarine, and use as is or as an ingredient in a recipe.

How to use: Carrots fit into every course in the menu. Appetizers of carrot juice, carrot soup, carrot curls on a relish tray, or carrot sticks for dips are colorful as well as stimulating to the appetite.

Salads are enhanced by crisp, cold, sweet bits of carrot. Raisins and carrots are a popular salad combination. Carrot slices and shreds are quite good in both tossed and gelatin salad recipes.

Pineapple-Carrot Toss

    1 8¾-ounce can pineapple
          tidbits, drained
    2 cups shredded carrots
    ½ cup plumped raisins
          Mayonnaise or salad dressing

Combine pineapple, carrots, and raisins. Chill thoroughly. Just before serving, add mayonnaise to moisten. Makes 6 servings.

Carrots frequently appear in the main dish of the menu. Casseroles and soufflés use them as a main ingredient or as a complementary flavor to the main food. Carrots and potatoes are traditionally cooked with pot roast. Garnishes of carrot zigzags, curls, and corkscrews are attractive on the main dish. Both the root and leaves can be used in stew.

Burgundy Beef Stew

  1 10¾-ounce can condensed
     tomato soup
  1 10½-ounce can condensed beef
     broth
  ½ cup red Burgundy
  3 tablespoons all-purpose flour
  ½ teaspoon dried basil leaves,
     crushed
       • • •
1½ pounds beef chuck, cut in
     1-inch cubes
  4 medium potatoes, peeled and
     halved
  4 medium carrots, quartered
  1 large onion, sliced

In a large saucepan combine tomato soup, beef broth, and Burgundy; blend in flour, 1 teaspoon salt, dash pepper, and basil. Add meat, potatoes, carrots, and onion; stir to distribute through gravy. Cover and simmer 1½ hours, stirring occasionally. Makes 6 servings.

As a side-dish vegetable in the main course, carrots go well with all meats. Simply boil the vegetable and season with salt and pepper—or with other herbs and spices, such as parsley, thyme, dill, cloves, ginger, mint, rosemary, and garlic. These add a different flavor combination. Carrots can be baked, mashed, glazed with honey or seasoned with lemon butter.

Bright, golden carrots

←Include vitamin-rich carrots in menus for their crisp texture, color, and sweet flavor. Raw or cooked they are low in calories.

Minted Carrots

  5 or 6 carrots
  2 tablespoons butter or margarine
  1 tablespoon honey
  2 teaspoons chopped fresh mint

Cut carrots in strips, cook in boiling salted water till tender, and drain. Combine butter or margarine, honey, and mint; heat till butter is melted. Add carrots; simmer till glazed, about 8 minutes. Makes 4 or 5 servings.

Desserts made from carrots are becoming more and more popular. Delicious cakes, pies, and puddings use carrots as a major ingredient for flavor and texture. Carrots are also great for nibbling between meals. (See also *Vegetable*.)

Carrot-Pineapple Cake

1½ cups sifted all-purpose flour
  1 cup sugar
  1 teaspoon baking powder
  1 teaspoon baking soda
  1 teaspoon ground cinnamon
  ⅔ cup salad oil
  2 eggs
  1 cup finely shredded carrot
  ½ cup crushed pineapple
     (with syrup)
  1 teaspoon vanilla
    Cream Cheese Frosting

Sift together into large mixing bowl flour, sugar, baking powder, soda, cinnamon, and ½ teaspoon salt. Add salad oil, eggs, carrot, pineapple, and vanilla. Mix till moistened; beat 2 minutes at medium speed on electric mixer.

Bake in greased and floured 9x9x2-inch pan at 350° about 35 minutes. Cool 10 minutes; remove from pan. Cool. Frost.

Cream Cheese Frosting: In small mixing bowl combine one 3-ounce package cream cheese, softened; 1 tablespoon butter or margarine, softened; and 1 teaspoon vanilla. Beat at low speed on electric mixer till light. Gradually add 2 cups sifted confectioners' sugar, beating till fluffy. If necessary, add milk to make of spreading consistency. Stir in ½ cup chopped pecans, if desired. Frosts one 9-inch cake.

Parslied Carrots

8 medium carrots
2 tablespoons water
2 tablespoons butter or margarine
1 teaspoon sugar
¼ teaspoon salt
Dash pepper
2 teaspoons snipped parsley

Peel carrots; halve lengthwise. Place in 10x6x1½-inch baking dish. Add water, butter or margarine, sugar, salt, and pepper. Cover tightly with foil. Bake at 400° till tender, about 45 to 50 minutes. Sprinkle with parsley before serving. Makes 4 to 6 servings.

Skillet Carrots

Melt 3 tablespoons butter in skillet. Add 8 medium carrots, coarsely shredded. Sprinkle with ½ teaspoon salt. Cover and cook till tender, 5 to 8 minutes. Top with snipped parsley.

Sprinkle snipped parsley over baked carrots to dress up a vegetable dish. Parslied Carrots are suitable for oven meal menus.

Spicy Carrot Sticks

2 tablespoons butter or margarine
1 teaspoon cornstarch
½ cup water
4 whole cloves
2 bay leaves
8 medium carrots, cut in thin
    strips (about 4 cups)

Melt butter in saucepan and blend in cornstarch. Add water. Cook, stirring constantly, until mixture is thickened. Add 1 teaspoon salt, dash pepper, cloves, bay leaves, and carrots. Cover pan and simmer till carrots are tender, about 10 to 12 minutes. Remove cloves and bay leaves. Makes 6 servings.

Golden Carrot Bake

3 cups shredded carrots
2 cups cooked rice
6 ounces process American
    cheese, shredded (1½ cups)
½ cup milk
2 beaten eggs
2 tablespoons minced onion
1 teaspoon salt
¼ teaspoon pepper
2 ounces process American
    cheese, shredded (½ cup)

Combine carrots, rice, 1½ cups cheese, milk, and eggs. Stir in onion, salt, and pepper. Pour mixture into a greased 1½-quart casserole dish. Sprinkle the ½ cup cheese over top. Bake at 350° for 50 to 60 minutes. Makes 6 servings.

Carrots Supreme

1 tablespoon butter or margarine
1 cup sliced carrots
1 cup bias-sliced celery
½ cup green pepper strips
Dash dried dillweed

Melt butter in heavy skillet; add carrots, celery, and green pepper. Cover and cook over medium heat 7 minutes. Season with ½ teaspoon salt, dash pepper, and dillweed. Cook over low heat till vegetables are just tender, about 5 minutes. Makes 3 or 4 servings.

Carrots Lyonnaise

Made with a French flair—

　1　**pound carrots (6 medium)**
　1　**chicken bouillon cube**
　½　**cup boiling water**
　　　　• • •
　¼　**cup butter or margarine**
　3　**medium onions, sliced**
　1　**tablespoon all-purpose flour**
　¼　**teaspoon salt**
　　　Dash pepper
　¾　**cup water**
　　　Sugar

Peel carrots and cut in julienne strips. Dissolve bouillon cube in the ½ cup boiling water. Cook carrots in bouillon, covered, 10 minutes. In saucepan melt butter; add onions and cook, covered, 15 minutes, stirring occasionally. Stir in flour, salt, pepper, and the ¾ cup water; bring to boiling. Add carrots and bouillon; simmer, uncovered, 10 minutes. Add pinch of sugar. Makes 6 servings.

Summertime Carrots

　2　**cups sliced carrots**
　¼　**cup beef broth**
　1　**teaspoon cornstarch**
　2　**tablespoons sauterne**
　1　**cup seedless green grapes**
　1　**tablespoon butter or margarine**
　½　**teaspoon lemon juice**
　¼　**teaspoon salt**

Cook carrots in beef broth till crisp-tender, 8 to 10 minutes. Blend cornstarch with sauterne; stir into carrots. Add grapes, butter, lemon juice, salt, and dash pepper. Cook and stir just till mixture comes to boiling. Serves 4.

Glazed Carrots

In skillet heat ⅓ cup brown sugar and 2 tablespoons butter till sugar dissolves. Add 8 cooked carrots (whole or halved lengthwise); cook over medium heat, turning carrots till well glazed and tender, about 12 minutes.

Dramatize vegetables with a smidgen of sugar, a tang of orange, or a hint of onion. Fine examples are Carrots Lyonnaise and Orange-Glazed Baby Beets. (See *Beet* for recipe.)

CARVING —Cutting meat, fish, or poultry into slices or pieces for serving.

Carving was one of the first dining arts to be refined. From ancient Roman days until the Elizabethan era, men of high rank were the official carvers. However, for a short period, women did do some of the carving as well as other hostess chores. The idea of paper frills on poultry and meat is a direct carry-over from those days when they were used to protect the lady's fingers from greasy meat. This woman's role, however, soon reverted back to the men. Today, carving is considered the man's domain, although it's quite acceptable for women to carve.

Carving serves an important function for both the food and the dining atmosphere. Meat correctly carved, is more attractive and more appetizing. The flavor is better because the juices do not flow out. More servings are available with less waste —making the meat more economical.

A dramatic atmosphere can be achieved by carving at the table. This is a ceremony which the host can rightfully be proud to perform and guests honored to witness.

However, if the host is carving and he is not experienced or confident in his carving abilities, the hostess should carry on a conversation with the guests. This will help divert some of the attention away from the carver while he carves.

Basic equipment: For carving, one needs the food, platter, knife, fork, and steel.

The meat must be properly prepared. Have the meatman saw the bones, especially the backbone, or remove the bones entirely. The absence of bones simplifies the job. Do not overcook the meat or it will fall apart when you slice. Let a roast stand 10 to 20 minutes before carving so the meat can firm up. It's not necessary to let steaks and chops stand. Cover the roast loosely with a piece of foil to keep it warm. Remove strings and skewers. However, leave a few strings on a rolled roast so it won't unroll when carved.

Place the meat on a platter which is suitable for carving. A wooden one is best since it does not dull the knife. Also, there are specially designed platters with spikes to hold the meat in place.

Sharp knives are essential for easy carving. Select an electric knife or standard hollow-ground knife with a sturdy well-riveted handle. Choose a knife or set for its good blade and construction rather than for decorative handles. Use a fork to hold meat steady while cutting. Some forks even have guards which protect the hand. The tines are sharp and vary in width for the intended purpose.

You need several knives and forks for carving: (1) An 11-inch knife with a straight edge and narrow blade and a fork with wide tines for a large roast, ham, sirloin, or rib roast. (2) An eight- or nine-inch knife with curved blade, and a fork with narrow tines, for medium and small roasts and legs of lamb. (3) A six- or seven-inch curved-edge knife and a fork with narrow tines for steaks, chops, and poultry.

You also need a steel or another knife sharpener to keep the blade true and sharp.

Basic techniques: The stage must be set properly for easy carving, whether it be done in the kitchen or at the table.

The carver must know the anatomy of the meat—the location of the bones and how the grain runs. Striking a bone accidentally dulls the knife and can possibly knock over the meat. The cutting is usually done across grain. (Grain is the long fibers.) Cutting across the grain makes meat easier to chew and juicier. But when grain is not easy to determine, follow the meatman's original cut.

Arrange the meat on a platter which is large enough to hold it and the slices— or provide another plate for the slices. Avoid excessive garnishes or vegetables on the meat platter which can get in the way or get knocked off during carving.

Now you can (as the carver) begin the ceremony which, of course, has been well rehearsed before presenting before guests. Sharpen the knife with the steel, firmly insert the fork, and slice with steady, firm strokes. Keep the knife angle the same so the slices will be uniform. Stack slices until enough is carved for one round of servings. This keeps the slices warm during carving. Place servings on warmed plates. Don't forget to divide and serve garnishes, vegetables, or stuffings, also.

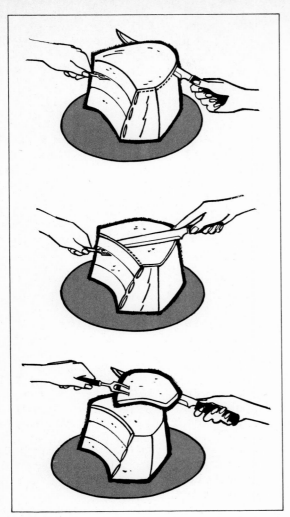

Flank steak, *below*, is held on board with fork; start cutting at narrow end. Hold knife blade at an angle parallel to board.

Cut remaining meat in very thin slices at the same angle. Carving this way cuts with the grain of the flank steak.

Standing rib roast, *above*, is carved with large end down. Insert fork between ribs. Cut across grain from the fat side to rib bone.

Use tip of knife to cut along rib bones to loosen each slice. Keep as close to bones as possible to make the largest servings.

To lift slice off roast, slide the knife under the slice and steady it with the fork on top. Arrange slices on heated serving platter.

Slice beef brisket, *right*, across grain, ⅛ to ¼ inch thick. Carve from two sides since grain goes in several directions.

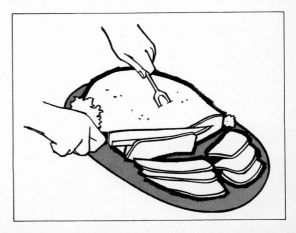

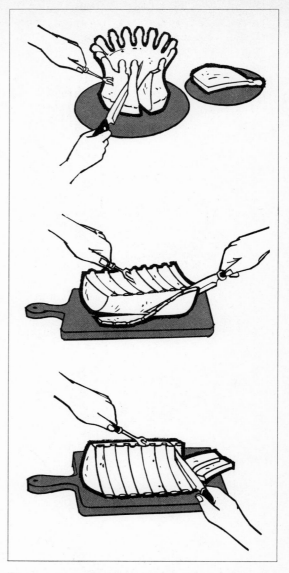

Ham or leg of lamb is carved with shank end on carver's right. Cut a few slices from bottom; wedge slices underneath to steady.

Remove any stuffing from crown roast. Insert fork between ribs. Carve between ribs beginning where ribs are tied together.

Starting at shank end, cut out and remove small wedge. Slices are then carved perpendicular to the long horizontal leg bone.

Remove backbone from pork blade loin roast, leaving as much meat on roast as possible. Turn bone side toward carver.

Release meat slices by running knife along the leg bone, starting at shank end. Turn the roast on its side and cut additional slices as they are needed.

Insert fork in top of the roast. Cut meat servings close along each side of the rib bone. One slice will contain a piece of bone, the next meat slice will be boneless.

Place turkey on board with wing tips folded back. Pull leg out. Cut through meat between thigh and back. Disjoint leg.

For leg, slice meat parallel to bone and under some of the tendons, turning leg. Arrange slices on heated serving platter.

Make a deep horizontal cut into the breast close to wing before carving white meat.

Cut slices from top down to the horizontal cut. Repeat steps with other side of the bird.

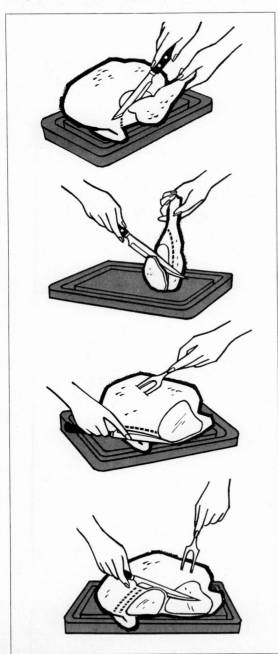

CASABA *(kuh sä' buh)*—A winter muskmelon. The mild, sweet casaba is large, globe-shaped, and pointed at the stem end.

Casaba melons are named after the Turkish town of Kassaba which first exported them. The melons in American markets are from California and Arizona.

How to select: Casaba is ripe when the rind is a buttery-yellow color. There should be a softening at the blossom end. The melons are most abundant July to November. Avoid melons with dark, sunken water-soaked spots. They are decaying.

How to store: Leave melons at room temperature if not ripe. Store ripe ones in the refrigerator sealed in a container or in clear plastic wrap. Whole melons keep a week; pieces keep two to four days.

How to prepare: Split casaba open, remove seeds, and slice or cut into pieces of desired size. Chill in the refrigerator.

Casaba melons have soft, creamy-white meat enclosed in a tough, wrinkled, buttery-yellow rind. They have little or no aroma.

How to use: Serve melon as an appetizer, salad, snack, or dessert. Also, use pieces in combination salads. Serve chilled (but not ice cold) with salt, a lemon wedge, or lime wedge. (See also *Melon.*)

Chicken and Ham Salad

  1⅓ cups uncooked long-grain rice
  ¼ cup French salad dressing
  ¾ cup mayonnaise
  1 tablespoon finely chopped green onion with tops
  ½ to 1 teaspoon curry powder
  ½ teaspoon dry mustard
  ¾ cup cooked chicken *or* turkey cut in julienne strips
  ¾ cup fully cooked ham cut in julienne strips
  1 cup sliced raw cauliflower
  ½ 10-ounce package frozen peas, cooked, drained, and chilled
  ½ cup chopped celery
  ½ cup thinly sliced radishes
  1 casaba melon, well chilled

Cook rice according to package directions; toss with French dressing and chill several hours. Combine mayonnaise, onion, ½ teaspoon salt, dash pepper, curry, and mustard. Add to chilled rice and toss. Add chicken, ham, cauliflower, peas, celery, and radishes; toss.

Using sawtooth cut, halve casaba melon; remove seeds. With grapefruit knife or large sharp-edged spoon, loosen melon meat from rind. Slice meat of each melon half into sections so it can be served with the salad. Fill melon halves with salad. Makes 6 servings.

CASEIN *(kā′ sēn)*—A protein found only in milk. Eighty percent of the protein in milk consists of casein. Acid or rennet causes casein to coagulate and form a curd which is the basis for making cheeses.

Casaba doubles as a serving bowl

←Begin mixing Chicken and Ham Salad a day ahead to save last-minute flurry. This main dish is hearty enough to please the men.

CASHEW NUT *(kash′ o͞o)*—A small, kidney-shaped nut. Cashew is native to India, Africa, and tropical America. These nuts are the seeds of an applelike fruit which grows on an evergreen tree. Unlike other nuts, they do not have shells.

Today, cashew nuts are imported mainly from India and Brazil. They are sold roasted and salted in cellophane bags, cans, and jars. The nuts can be stored in tightly covered containers in a refrigerator for six months, or in a freezer for one year.

Cashew nuts are ideal for eating out-of-hand as snacks or with drinks. Use as flavor accents or garnishes in salad, casserole, candy, frosting, chicken, and curry. Each nut adds 11 to 14 calories to the daily diet. (See also *Nut.*)

Frosted Cashew Drops

  ½ cup butter or margarine
  1 cup brown sugar
  1 egg
  ½ teaspoon vanilla
     • • •
  2 cups sifted all-purpose flour
  ¾ teaspoon baking soda
  ¾ teaspoon baking powder
  ½ teaspoon ground cinnamon
  ¼ teaspoon ground nutmeg
  ⅓ cup dairy sour cream
  1 cup salted cashew nuts, broken
    Golden Butter Icing

Cream butter and sugar. Add egg and vanilla; beat well. Sift together flour, soda, baking powder, ¼ teaspoon salt, cinnamon, and nutmeg. Add to creamed mixture alternately with sour cream. Stir in nuts. Drop from teaspoon, 2 inches apart, on greased cookie sheet. Bake at 400° till lightly browned, about 8 to 10 minutes. Remove at once from pan. Cool and frost with Golden Butter Icing. Makes 48 cookies.

Golden Butter Icing: Heat and stir 3 tablespoons butter till browned. Slowly beat in 2 cups sifted confectioners' sugar, 2 tablespoons milk, and 1 teaspoon vanilla.

CASSAVA *(kuh sä′ vuh)*—A shrub and the roots of this shrub. Tapioca is made with the starch removed from the root.

CASSEROLE

*One-dish combinations for a satisfying
main course or hearty meat accompaniment.*

Casserole is the name given to both a type of baking dish with a cover and the food that is baked or served in it. In common usage, especially in the United States, any one-dish meal is called a casserole even though it may actually be cooked in a skillet or kettle and transferred to a casserole dish for serving at the table.

The word casserole is derived from *casse*, an early French word for a small pan. It is from this background that foods listed on a menu as being served "en casserole" are single portions in individual dishes such as a ramekin or other small ovenproof container. Larger family-style casseroles contain several servings.

Casserole cooking has been done since man first learned to make earthenware pottery that would withstand the burning coals of an open fire or the heat of a primitive oven. It was natural to prepare satisfying one-dish meals by combining chunks of meat with grasses, herbs, wild fruits, and vegetables. Water was added to prevent the foods from sticking. Man soon discovered that simmering the meat made it tender and juicy. Later, when the earthenware pot had a cover, the liquid did not boil away as quickly and left man with a tasty broth to serve with the meat. This was an early form of stew which today is often served "en casserole." As the years went by, the seasonings in the broth became just as important as the other foods in the stew. As the art of sauce making

developed, the many variations of broth found their place as a necessary ingredient in moistening and seasoning meats, fish, and vegetables in casserole dishes. And, as you know, today many nationalities have special seasoning combinations which have been passed down from mother to daughter for generations.

Choosing the container

Earthenware casseroles of assorted shapes and sizes are still popular for one-dish meals. However, be sure that they are ovenproof. Some types of pottery do not stand up well under sudden contrasts in temperature. Thus, earthenware casseroles are often used as a final serving dish rather than as the actual cooking utensil.

The covered baking dish is the classic casserole in use today. Made of ovenproof glass or ceramic material, it has a close-fitting lid. Some casseroles fit into a frame to hold the dish while serving at the table. Common sizes for this basic glass dish are 10x6x1½ inches (1½ quarts), 12x7½x2 inches (2 quarts), and 13x9x2 inches (3 quarts). Volume and dimensions are usually marked on the bottom of the utensil.

Many skillets are designed for both top-of-the range and oven cooking. If the casserole is to be placed in the oven, the skillet handle should be of heatproof material or be detachable. An electric skillet should not be overlooked as a container. It has one added advantage in that it can be used to prepare food right at the table. Many are colorful and attractive enough for a company buffet meal.

As a rule of thumb, practically any heatproof container makes a satisfactory casserole. If it does not have a lid of its own, you can use aluminum foil. Most recipes

Here's a trio of meaty casseroles

← Burger Skillet Stew features juicy meatballs. Bavarian-Style Stew adds red cabbage. Pioneer Beef Stew wears a pastry top.

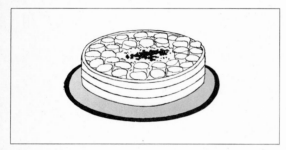

Lemon wedges (top) form a golden star atop a seafood casserole. To add more color, dip points in paprika or snipped parsley.

Pinwheel (middle) hot cooked asparagus or overlap slices of green pepper, onion, or tomatoes atop ham or chicken dishes.

Ring top (bottom) with biscuits or dumplings when mixture is bubbly hot. This assures topper will be thoroughly cooked.

specify the size of dish needed. It is a simple matter to measure the volume of a particular pan or dish. Just count the number of cupfuls of water needed to fill it. Or, compare the surface area of two pans, by measuring the length and width from the inside edges. Multiplying width times length determines surface area in square inches. Remember that the type of baking container will influence the oven temperature or baking time. For example, when switching from a deep container to a shallow one of the same capacity, baking time is shorter for the shallower pan. Recipes generally refer to a baking *pan* when the utensil is metal, and a baking *dish* when it is glass. The reason for the distinction is that the oven temperature is 25° lower when baking in glass utensils.

Casserole combinations

You can prepare casseroles from either cooked or uncooked ingredients, or a combination of both. Generally, start stews with uncooked meat. Ground meats, especially beef, are basic to many types of casserole dishes. Vegetables, which you add later in the cooking time, may be fresh, frozen, or canned. Other recipes taking advantage of canned meats and seafood may rely on canned sauces and vegetables. This way you only need to heat the enticing mixture to blend flavors. Likewise, leftover cooked foods find their way into an assortment of oven-easy meals.

Since most casserole ingredients will be diced or cut up in bite-size pieces, the sauce you use to hold the mixture together is important as a binder. Variations of the classic white sauce are most often used. For convenience sake, you may base the sauce on a canned condensed cream soup such as celery, chicken, or mushroom.

If a white sauce is not compatible with the other foods you're serving, consider making a sauce from a thickened broth or gravy you get from the natural juices of the meat. If the casserole is large in volume, add a bouillon cube or canned broth to augment the sauce.

In a great many tasty casseroles, rice, noodles, macaroni, bread cubes, or potatoes are important ingredients. Their presence gives the dish its one-dish meal status because the starchy complement is included with the meat or cheese. In some cases they can extend the meat ingredient. However, never let the amount of these starch foods outweigh the proportion of the meat and vegetables in the casserole.

Since most casseroles are baked, give some thought to toppings which will brown nicely, yet prevent the surface of the food from drying out. Buttered crumbs, crushed cereal, or potato chips protect the surface and become toasty crisp when the casserole cover is removed during the last few minutes of the baking time.

If you like, add a fancy touch just before the casserole is served. It may be as simple as a few sprigs of parsley or a dash of paprika. Other easy decorating tricks are illustrated on these two pages.

Freezing casseroles

Main-dish casseroles carefully tucked away in the freezer and used within two to four months are work savers on a busy day. Although most meat, vegetable, and sauce combinations freeze well, certain cooking and seasoning tricks will improve the quality of the food.

Generally, it is most satisfactory to freeze the casserole before baking. Otherwise, you are really freezing a leftover which may or may not improve with another heating. In fact, it is wise not to overcook any foods that go into the casserole that require prepreparation. This is especially true of rice, noodles, macaroni, and spaghetti products. They will finish cooking during the time the food is heated before serving. Toppings such as crushed potato chips, crumbs, and cheese should be added near the end of baking time rather than going into the freezer.

It is wise to go easy on the seasonings in a casserole to be frozen. More can always be added later if necessary but some ingredients such as garlic, pepper, and celery intensify during freezing. Experienced cooks will reduce slightly the amounts called for in the recipe.

Use as little fat in the recipe being prepared for the freezer as possible. During reheating it may not blend smoothly.

Remember, a shallow dish will not take as long to thaw and bake as a deep one. If the baking dish is not used, select a freezer container with a wide-top opening so that it's unnecessary to completely thaw the food before removing it from the container for heating. An easy way to remove

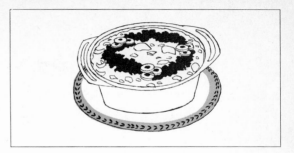

Wreathe the casserole (top) in snipped parsley. Place sliced pimiento-stuffed olives in clusters or scatter them over the surface.

Diagonally cut cheese slices (middle) make handy triangles. Point them towards the center or overlap them along the outer edge.

Spread toast with butter (bottom), then sprinkle with garlic salt. Cut toast in small cubes; place on hot casserole before serving.

frozen main dishes from glass canning-freezing jars is to let cool water run on the cap for two or three minutes. This is long enough for the surface of food touching the glass to thaw. Then remove the cap and invert the jar to let the food slide out into the pan to be used for reheating.

Only oven-proof containers can safely be transferred from freezer to hot oven. To save freezer space and free the dish for other use, line the casserole with heavy foil. Allow lengths of foil to extend beyond ends of pan. Fill, then fold the foil over food to seal. Freeze. Remove foil package from dish. Store in freezer. To heat, place in same baking dish, foil and all.

Main-dish meals

Casseroles appear most frequently as the main course of the meal. They may serve as a simple supper for the family or as one of the several entrées on a buffet table.

❧MENU❧

ORIENTAL LUNCHEON
Chopstick Veal Bake

Asparagus Spears   *Spiced Peaches*

Lemon Sherbet   *Ginger Bars*

Hot or *Iced Tea*

Chopstick Veal Bake

 1½ pounds veal steak, cut ½ inch
       thick
  2 tablespoons salad oil
  1 cup chopped onion
 1½ cups sliced celery
  1 cup diced green pepper
  3 tablespoons chopped canned
       pimiento
  ½ cup uncooked long-grain rice
  1 10½-ounce can condensed
       cream of mushroom soup
  1 cup milk
  2 tablespoons soy sauce
  1 3-ounce can chow mein noodles

Cut meat in 2x½-inch strips. Brown in hot oil. Add remaining ingredients *except* noodles. Turn into 2-quart casserole. Cover; bake at 350° for 1¼ to 1½ hours; stir occasionally. Last 5 minutes uncover; top with noodles. Serves 8.

Pioneer Beef Stew

  1 cup large dry lima beans
  1 teaspoon salt
  ¼ cup all-purpose flour
  1 teaspoon salt
  1 teaspoon pepper
  1 pound beef stew meat, cubed
  2 tablespoons shortening
  ½ cup chopped onion
 1½ cups tomato juice
  1 teaspoon salt
  1 small bay leaf
    Dash ground allspice
  1 medium onion, quartered
  3 medium carrots, cut in 1-inch
      slices
  3 stalks celery, cut in 1-inch
      slices
    Pastry Topper

Add beans to 2½ cups water and 1 teaspoon salt and soak overnight. (Or bring mixture to a boil; boil 2 minutes. Remove from heat; let stand covered 1 hour.) Combine flour, 1 teaspoon salt, and pepper in plastic bag; add meat and shake. Brown meat in hot shortening. Add chopped onion, tomato juice, 1 teaspoon salt, bay leaf, and allspice. Cover tightly; simmer 30 minutes. Add beans with liquid, onion, carrots, and celery. Cover, simmer till vegetables are tender, 45 minutes. Remove bay leaf. Thicken stew, if desired. Arrange baked Pastry Topper on hot stew. Serves 6.

Pastry Topper: Prepare 1 stick piecrust mix following package directions. Roll out to 8-inch circle, ¼ inch thick. Cut in 6 wedges. Prick with fork. Bake at 450° 12 to 15 minutes.

Bavarian-Style Stew

Brown 2 pounds beef chuck, cut in 1-inch cubes, in 2 tablespoons hot shortening. Add 3 cups water; 2 medium onions, sliced; 1 tablespoon salt; 1½ teaspoons caraway seed; ¼ teaspoon pepper; and 1 bay leaf. Cover; simmer 1 hour. Add ½ cup vinegar and 2 tablespoons sugar. Cut 1 small head red cabbage in thin wedges; place atop meat.

Cover; simmer till tender, 45 minutes. Remove cabbage to platter. Add ½ cup broken gingersnaps to liquid; bring to boiling, stirring constantly. Makes 6 to 8 servings.

Burger Skillet Stew

        1 beaten egg
     1/3 cup milk
     1/3 cup fine dry bread crumbs
        1 envelope spaghetti sauce mix
        1 pound ground beef
        1 tablespoon shortening
        4 medium carrots, peeled and
             cut in 1-inch pieces
     1/2 cup chopped green pepper
        1 medium onion, quartered
        1 10 3/4-ounce can beef gravy
     1/4 cup water

Combine egg, milk, bread crumbs, and *3 table-spoons* of the spaghetti sauce mix. Add ground beef; mix thoroughly. Form mixture into 12 balls; brown in a skillet in hot shortening.

Add carrot pieces, green pepper, and onion to skillet with the meatballs. Blend remaining spaghetti sauce mix with beef gravy and water; pour over meat and vegetables. Simmer, covered, till vegetables are tender, 50 to 60 minutes. Makes 4 to 6 servings.

Family Skillet Supper

     1/4 cup butter or margarine
        3 cups loose-pack frozen
             hash-brown potatoes
     1/4 cup chopped onion
     1/4 cup chopped green pepper
     1/4 teaspoon salt
             Dash pepper
        4 slightly beaten eggs
        1 12-ounce can luncheon meat
        2 ounces sharp process cheese,
             shredded (1/2 cup)

In 10-inch skillet melt butter. Add hash-brown potatoes, chopped onion, green pepper, salt, and pepper. Stir to combine. Cover; cook over low heat 15 minutes, stirring occasionally. Pour eggs evenly over top of potato mixture.

Cut luncheon meat in 3 1/2 x 3/4-inch sticks; arrange spoke fashion atop eggs. Cover skillet; cook mixture over low heat till eggs are set, about 10 minutes. Sprinkle with shredded cheese; cover till cheese is melted. Cut in wedges. Makes 5 or 6 servings.

Supper ready in 30 minutes? There's no trick to it when frozen hash-brown potatoes, canned luncheon meat, eggs, onion, and sharp cheese team up in a Family Skillet Supper.

Pastry triangles outline a Tuna-Vegetable Pie. Beneath the crust a creamy, herb-seasoned sauce brings together bright carrots and peas, snowy potato cubes, and delicate tuna.

Pork Chops in Spanish Rice

    5 pork chops, ½ inch thick
    2 tablespoons shortening
          . . .
    1 teaspoon salt
    ½ teaspoon chili powder
      Dash pepper
    ¾ cup uncooked long-grain rice
    ½ cup chopped onion
    ¼ cup chopped green pepper
    1 28-ounce can tomatoes
          . . .
    5 green pepper rings
    2 ounces sharp process American
      cheese, shredded (½ cup)

Trim excess fat from chops. In skillet slowly brown pork chops in melted shortening, about 15 to 20 minutes; drain off excess fat.

Combine salt, chili powder, and pepper; sprinkle over meat. Add rice, onion, and chopped green pepper. Pour tomatoes over. Cover and cook over low heat 35 minutes, stirring occasionally. Add green pepper rings and cook till rice and meat are tender, 5 minutes. Sprinkle with cheese. Makes 5 servings.

Tuna-Vegetable Pie

    1½ cups sliced carrots
    1½ cups peeled, cubed potatoes
     ¼ cup butter or margarine
     ¼ cup chopped onion
      2 tablespoons all-purpose flour
     ¼ teaspoon dried rosemary leaves,
        crushed
      1 8-ounce can peas, drained
      2 6½- or 7-ounce cans tuna,
        drained and flaked
      1 stick piecrust mix

Cook carrots and potatoes in small amount of boiling water till tender. Drain, reserving liquid. Add enough milk to make 2 cups.

Melt butter in saucepan. Add onion; cook till tender but not brown. Blend in flour, rosemary, ½ teaspoon salt, and dash pepper. Add milk mixture all at once. Cook, stirring constantly, till mixture is thick and bubbly.

Add vegetables and tuna. Turn into 10x6x 1½-inch dish. Prepare piecrust mix following package directions. Roll out; cut into 6 triangles. Place atop bubbly hot tuna mixture. Bake at 425° 30 to 35 minutes. Serves 6.

Triple Seafood Bake

Stir 1 cup milk, 1 cup light cream, and 1⁄3 cup dry sherry into one 10½-ounce can condensed cream of mushroom soup.

Add 1⅓ cups uncooked packaged precooked rice; one 4½- or 5-ounce can shrimp, drained and split lengthwise; one 5-ounce can lobster, drained and cut up; one 7½-ounce can minced clams, drained; one 5-ounce can water chestnuts, drained and sliced; one 3-ounce can sliced mushrooms, drained; 1 tablespoon parsley flakes; and ¼ teaspoon instant minced garlic. Turn into 2-quart casserole. Sprinkle with paprika and 2 tablespoons toasted sliced almonds. Dot with 2 tablespoons butter. Bake at 350° for 50 minutes. Makes 6 servings.

Ham Medley

     1 cup chopped celery
     ½ cup chopped green pepper
     ½ cup chopped onion
     ¼ cup butter or margarine, melted
     ¼ cup all-purpose flour
    2½ cups milk
     3 cups cream-style cottage cheese
     4 cups fully cooked ham cut in
        ½-inch cubes
     1 8-ounce package noodles, cooked
        and drained
     2 tablespoons butter or margarine
     ½ cup fine dry bread crumbs

Cook vegetables in butter. Blend in flour, ½ teaspoon salt, and dash pepper. Stir in milk and cheese; cook and stir till boiling. Stir in ham and noodles; turn into 3-quart casserole. Combine remaining ingredients; sprinkle over. Bake at 350° 1 hour. Serves 10 to 12.

Chicken Chow Bake

Combine 2 cups diced cooked chicken; one 10½-ounce can condensed cream of mushroom soup; one 8¾-ounce can pineapple tidbits, drained; 1 cup thinly sliced celery; 2 tablespoons chopped green onion; and 1 teaspoon soy sauce. Add *1 cup* of a 3-ounce can chow mein noodles. Turn mixture into 1½-quart casserole. Top with remaining noodles. Bake at 350° till hot, 45 minutes. Pass soy sauce. Serves 4 to 6.

Macaroni-Cheese Puff

     ½ cup small elbow macaroni
    1½ cups milk
     6 ounces sharp process American
        cheese, shredded
     3 tablespoons butter or margarine
     3 eggs, separated
     1 cup soft bread crumbs
     ¼ cup chopped canned pimiento
     1 tablespoon snipped parsley
     1 tablespoon grated onion
     ¼ teaspoon cream of tartar

Cook macaroni in boiling salted water till tender; drain. Combine milk, cheese, and butter. Cook and stir over low heat till cheese is melted. Beat egg yolks. Stir small amount of hot mixture into beaten yolks. Return to hot mixture; blend thoroughly. Add cooked macaroni, crumbs, pimiento, parsley, and onion.

Beat egg whites with cream of tartar till stiff peaks form. Fold gently into macaroni mixture. Pour into *ungreased* 1½-quart soufflé dish. Bake at 325° till set, about 1 hour. Serves 6.

Side-dish casseroles

Vegetable combinations baked in a casserole bring variety to the menu. Cooked in the oven, they are perfect companions for roasts or braised meats. Butter-baked rice is a pleasing change from baked potatoes to serve with steak or chicken. Experimenting with herbs to season the rice expands the flavor possibilities. Thyme, rosemary, or marjoram head the list, but oregano, curry powder, or saffron can add a foreign influence.

❧MENU❧

SUNDAY CHICKEN DINNER
Perfect Fried Chicken
Baked Rice   Tomato-Zucchini Scallop
Relish Assortment
Chocolate Sundae
Beverage

Baked Rice

2 teaspoons salt
1 cup uncooked long-grain rice
⅓ cup butter or margarine
  Dash garlic salt
1 13¾-ounce can chicken
    broth *or* 2 chicken bouillon
    cubes dissolved in 1¾
    cups boiling water
  Finely snipped parsley
¼ cup toasted slivered almonds

Combine salt and 2 cups water; bring to boiling and pour over rice. Let stand 30 minutes. Rinse rice with cold water; drain. Melt butter in skillet. Add rice, and cook and stir over medium heat, stirring frequently, till butter is almost absorbed, about 5 minutes. Turn into 1-quart casserole; sprinkle with garlic salt. Pour the broth over the casserole mixture. Bake, covered, at 325° for 45 minutes. Add parsley; fluff with fork. Sprinkle with nuts. Bake, uncovered, 10 minutes. Serves 6 to 8.

Corn and Potato Scallop

1 17-ounce can whole kernel
    corn, drained
1 10¼-ounce can frozen cream
    of potato soup, thawed
¼ teaspoon salt
  Dash pepper
2 tablespoons butter or margarine
¼ cup shredded Parmesan cheese

Combine corn, soup, salt, and pepper. Turn into greased 1-quart casserole. Dot with butter or margarine; sprinkle Parmesan cheese over top. Bake at 325° until heated through, about 25 minutes. Makes 4 to 6 servings.

Lima-Cheese Bake

Pour boiling water over one 10-ounce package frozen lima beans; break apart. Drain. Blend one 11-ounce can condensed Cheddar cheese soup and ½ cup milk. Add limas, ¾ cup sliced celery, and ¼ cup snipped parsley. Stir in *half* of one 3½-ounce can French-fried onions. Bake at 350° for 35 minutes. Trim with remaining onions; bake 10 minutes. Makes 6 servings.

Tomato-Zucchini Scallop

2 small zucchini squash, sliced
1 medium onion, thinly sliced
2 small tomatoes, peeled and
    sliced
1 cup plain croutons
1 teaspoon salt
  Pepper
        • • •
1 tomato, cut in wedges
4 ounces sharp natural Cheddar
    cheese, shredded (1 cup)

In a 1½-quart casserole, layer *half* of the zucchini, onion, sliced tomatoes, and croutons. Season with ½ *teaspoon* of the salt and dash pepper. Repeat layers. Top with tomato wedges. Cover and bake at 350° for 1 hour. Uncover and sprinkle with cheese. Return to oven till cheese melts. Serve in sauce dishes. Makes 6 servings.

Festive Celery Casserole

4 cups celery cut in ¼-inch slices
2 tablespoons butter or margarine
1 10½-ounce can condensed cream
    of celery soup
2 tablespoons milk
2 tablespoons chopped canned
    pimiento
        • • •
½ cup finely crushed round cheese
    crackers (12 crackers)
1 tablespoon butter or margarine,
    melted

In a saucepan cook celery, covered, in the 2 tablespoons butter till tender, 15 to 20 minutes. Stir in soup, milk, and chopped pimiento. Pour into a 1-quart casserole.

Combine cracker crumbs and melted butter or margarine. Sprinkle crumb mixture over casserole. Bake at 350° for 30 minutes or till heated through. Makes 4 to 6 servings.

Oven-easy vegetables

Look to the oven for tempting vegetables →
such as Tomato-Zucchini Scallop and Stuffed Acorn Squash. (See *Acorn Squash* for recipe.)

CASSIA *(kash' uh, kas' ē-)* — A name used in the spice trade for several varieties of cinnamon bark native to China, Indo-China, and Indonesia. The buds and flowers are sometimes used in pickling.

Cassia is also a generic term for certain leguminous plants possessing medicinal properties. (See also *Cinnamon*.)

CASSOULET *(ka suh lā')* — A casserole specialty of the Toulouse region of France. The basic ingredient is stewed white beans to which pork, lamb, duck, and special sausages are added. Except for the white beans, the other ingredients differ in kind and amount in various towns.

CASTOR SUGAR — The British name to designate finely granulated sugar.

CATFISH — A freshwater fish native to the lakes and streams of the Great Lakes region and the Mississippi river with its many tributaries. The whiskerlike sensory barbels on the jaws lend the name catfish. Though the fish may weigh more than 100 pounds, average market size is from one to 20 pounds, dressed, ready-to-cook.

Catfish meat is firm and flaky with a delicate flavor. The small-sized panfish are favorites of anglers, but catfish are important commercially, too. Bullhead, channel, blue, or yellow catfish are names by which the fish is known. (See also *Fish*.)

CATSUP, CATCHUP, KETCHUP — A spicy, thick, slightly-sweet sauce served with meat and fish or used an an ingredient in main dishes. The most familiar is tomato. It may have a smoke or other flavoring.

Best Tomato Catsup

  1½ teaspoon whole cloves
  1½ inches broken stick cinnamon
    1 teaspoon celery seed
    1 cup white vinegar

       · · ·

    8 pounds tomatoes, cored and
       quartered (about 25 medium)
    1 medium onion, chopped
  ¼ teaspoon cayenne pepper
    1 cup sugar

In small saucepan combine cloves, stick cinnamon, celery seed, and white vinegar. Cover; bring to a boil. Remove from heat; let stand. In a large kettle combine tomatoes, onion, and cayenne. Bring to boil; cook 15 minutes, stirring occasionally. Sieve mixture.

Add sugar to tomato juice. Bring to boil; *simmer* briskly till mixture is reduced by half (measure depth with ruler at start and end) about 1½ to 2 hours. Strain spice-vinegar mixture into tomato mixture; discard spices. Add 4 teaspoons salt. Simmer till of desired consistency, about 30 minutes. Stir often.

Fill hot pint jars to within ½ inch of top; adjust lids. Process in boiling water bath 5 minutes (count time after water returns to the boiling point). Makes 2 pints.

Sweet-Sour Stew

    2 pounds beef stew meat, cubed
  ¼ cup all-purpose flour
  ¼ cup shortening
  ½ cup catsup
  ¼ cup brown sugar
  ¼ cup vinegar
    1 tablespoon Worcestershire sauce
    1 teaspoon salt
    1 cup chopped onion
    6 large carrots, cut in
      ¾-inch pieces

Coat meat with mixture of flour, 1 teaspoon salt, and dash pepper. In large skillet brown meat well in hot shortening. Combine 1 cup water, catsup, brown sugar, vinegar, Worcestershire, and salt. Stir into browned meat; add onion. Cover; cook over low heat for 45 minutes, stirring occasionally. Add carrots. Cook till meat and carrots are tender, about 45 minutes. Makes 6 to 8 servings.

CAUDLE — A hot spiced drink given in past years to invalids. The recipe is English in origin and has numerous variations. One such variation consists of strong tea diluted with wine, to which spices are added. The concoction is further enriched with beaten egg yolk. Another variation with a base of cereal gruel makes use of beer or wine, sugar, and spices and is made either with or without egg.

CAULIFLOWER—A vegetable of the cabbage family having a compact, creamy white head, called a curd. Made up of tight clusters of flower buds, the curd is ready for eating before these buds open. The curd is surrounded with large green leaves. The outer leaves are often pinned or tied over the curd to help keep out foreign materials and to bleach or whiten the head as it matures. Although the curd is the part usually eaten, the leaves and stems can also be cooked and used in soups.

The name cauliflower comes from the Latin words *caulis* meaning stem, stalk, or cabbage, and *floris* meaning flower. Cauliflower has been used for many centuries—the earliest date around the sixth century B.C. in the Mediterranean area. The Italians have cultivated this vegetable since the 1500's. Through the years they have developed several cauliflower varieties including small green- or purple-headed types different from the common white-headed vegetable found in grocery stores.

Cauliflower became popular throughout Europe and eventually was brought to America. For about 200 years it was grown in this country almost exclusively by Italian families in New England. Since the 1920's, however, cauliflower has been grown widely in the United States; California, New York, Oregon, and Washington are the main producers. Because cauliflower thrives in moist climates with warm days and cool nights, the majority of the cauliflower crop comes from California.

Nutritional value: Here is an excellent source of vitamin C, especially when eaten raw: one cup of uncooked cauliflower meets the day's requirements for an adult. For those counting calories cauliflower is a must. One cup of cauliflower, raw or cooked, contains about 25 calories.

How to select: Overall appearance is the most helpful quality indicator for selecting cauliflower. Look for a head of cauliflower that is clean, heavy, and compact. It should have white or creamy white flowerets and a bright green jacket of leaves. Head size does not affect the quality, and leaves that sometimes grow through the curd may be ignored.

Avoid a cauliflower head that has many brown bruises, a speckled appearance, or if its leaves are yellowed or withered. Also avoid cauliflower that is beginning to break apart. These are all indications that the head has "passed its prime."

The peak season for cauliflower is from September through November. It can, however, be found in markets throughout the year. As purchased in the supermarket, it usually has most of its jacket leaves removed and often is covered in a clear wrapper. You can plan on four to six servings from a head of cauliflower that weighs 2½ to 3 pounds. Frozen cauliflower with or without a cheese sauce can be purchased year-round.

How to store: Keep fresh cauliflower refrigerated. To retard the wilting of green leaves, sprinkle with water then cover the head tightly in foil, clear plastic wrap, or place in a covered container.

To freeze, wash it thoroughly and cut into flowerets or pieces one inch thick. Blanch in boiling water for three minutes. Then chill in ice water three minutes and drain well. Pack tightly in moisture-vapor-proof containers. Seal, label with contents and date, then freeze. Generally, 1⅓ pounds cleaned and trimmed cauliflower yields about one pint when frozen.

How to prepare: Cauliflower may be cooked whole or broken first into flowerets. Or, simply wash and eat—uncooked.

To prepare, remove leaves and some of the woody stem. Cook, covered, in a small amount of boiling salted water until the cauliflower is just tender when tested with a fork. Generally, the whole head will cook in 20 to 25 minutes and flowerets in 10 to 15 minutes. Overcooking, even for only a few minutes, causes the vegetable to turn dark and the flavor to become strong and unpleasant, so test frequently.

How to use: This is a truly versatile and delicious vegetable. For example, include raw cauliflower flowerets as vegetable dippers on a platter of appetizers. Cauliflower and well-seasoned sour cream or cream cheese dips make excellent companions on your hors d'oeuvre tray.

Cauliflower makes a delicious addition to salads and adds an unusual crispness. Some flowerets are cooked while others are added to the salad uncooked.

Cauliflower-Ham Salad

  1 medium head cauliflower, broken
     into flowerets
  2 cups fully-cooked ham cut in
     strips
  ½ cup thin radish slices
  ½ cup sliced celery
  ½ cup mayonnaise or salad dressing
  2 tablespoons milk
  1 teaspoon sugar
  2 teaspoons prepared horseradish
    Lettuce cups

In a saucepan cook flowerets, covered, in a small amount of boiling salted water for 10 to 15 minutes; drain thoroughly. Toss with ham, radish slices, and celery; chill.

For dressing stir together mayonnaise or salad dressing, milk, sugar, and horseradish. Spoon cauliflower-ham mixture into lettuce cups and serve with dressing. Makes 6 servings.

Cauliflower Vinaigrette

  1 medium head cauliflower, broken
     into flowerets
  ⅔ cup salad oil
  ¼ cup white wine vinegar
  1 large tomato, chopped
  ⅓ cup chopped pimiento-stuffed
     green olives
  2 tablespoons chopped green onion
  1 tablespoon pickle relish
  1 teaspoon salt
  1 teaspoon paprika
  ⅛ teaspoon pepper

Cook flowerets, covered, in small amount of boiling salted water till just crisp-tender, about 10 minutes. Drain; place in shallow dish.

Combine oil, vinegar, tomato, olives, onion, relish, salt, paprika, and pepper. Pour over cauliflower; chill 2 to 3 hours. At serving time drain off excess oil and vinegar. Serve in lettuce-lined bowl and garnish with tomato wedges, if desired. Makes 8 to 10 servings.

Tangy Cauliflower Salad

  1 medium head cauliflower, broken
     into flowerets (about 4 cups)
  2 medium carrots, cut in julienne
     strips (1 cup)
  ⅓ cup French salad dressing
       • • •
  ½ ounce blue cheese, crumbled
     (2 tablespoons)
    Lettuce cups
  1 small avocado, peeled and
     sliced

Cut flowerets in half lengthwise. Combine cauliflower and carrot strips; toss with French dressing. Cover and refrigerate till ready to serve, stirring once or twice.

At serving time, sprinkle with blue cheese. Toss lightly and serve in crisp lettuce cups. Top each serving with avocado slices. Serves 6.

Cheese and cauliflower are natural go-togethers. A hot soup made with cheese, cauliflower, and broth is a gourmet's delight. Serve it as a main dish or as an appetizer soup.

Creamy Cauliflower Soup

  1 medium head cauliflower, broken
     into flowerets
  ¼ cup chopped onion
  ¼ cup butter or margarine
  ¼ cup all-purpose flour
  3 cups chicken broth
  2 cups milk
  1 teaspoon Worcestershire sauce
  4 ounces sharp process American
     cheese, shredded (1 cup)
    Snipped chives

Cook flowerets, covered, in small amount of boiling salted water till tender, 10 to 15 minutes; drain and coarsely chop.

In large saucepan cook onion in butter till tender but not brown. Blend in flour. Add chicken broth, milk, and Worcestershire sauce. Cook and stir till mixture thickens slightly. Add cauliflower. Bring to boiling and stir in cheese. Sprinkle each serving with snipped chives. Makes 6 to 8 servings.

Summer Scramble

2 tablespoons butter or margarine
½ cup chopped onion
1 small clove garlic, crushed
¼ cup snipped parsley
1 teaspoon salt
1 teaspoon seasoned salt
  Dash pepper
  Dash dried thyme leaves,
    crushed
1 medium head cauliflower, broken
    into small flowerets
3 large tomatoes, diced
2 small zucchini, sliced

In a large saucepan melt butter or margarine; cook onion and garlic until tender but not brown. Add remaining ingredients. Cover tightly. Simmer 15 to 20 minutes; uncover and cook about 10 minutes longer. Serve in sauce dishes with juice. Makes 10 servings.

For a change of pace prepare cauliflower for the vegetable course at your next meal. Here's a simple vegetable accompaniment: top cooked cauliflower with melted butter, then dash very lightly with nutmeg. Or, drizzle browned butter atop cooked cauliflower. (See also *Vegetable*.)

Crisp-cooked cauliflower marinates in a tangy salad dressing several hours before Cauliflower Vinaigrette is ready to serve. Plump tomato wedges arranged on top add a perky note.

Cheese Frosted Cauliflower

1 medium head cauliflower
Salt
½ cup mayonnaise or salad
  dressing
2 teaspoons prepared mustard
3 ounces sharp process American
  cheese, shredded (¾ cup)

Remove leaves and trim base from cauliflower. Wash. Cook whole, covered, in boiling salted water for 12 to 15 minutes. Drain. Place in *ungreased* shallow baking pan. Sprinkle with salt.

Combine mayonnaise and mustard; spread over cauliflower. Top with cheese. Bake at 375° till cheese is melted and bubbly, about 10 minutes. Makes 4 or 5 servings.

Cauliflower and Dilly Shrimp

1 medium head cauliflower
        . . .
2 tablespoons butter or margarine
2 tablespoons all-purpose flour
½ teaspoon dried dillweed
¼ teaspoon salt
Dash pepper
1¼ cups milk
1 cup cleaned cooked shrimp,
  cut up

Cook whole cauliflower, covered, in small amount of boiling salted water till tender, about 15 to 20 minutes; drain well.

Meanwhile in a small saucepan melt butter over low heat. Blend in flour, dillweed, salt, and pepper. Add milk all at once. Cook and stir till thickened and bubbly. Add shrimp; heat through. Place hot cauliflower on serving plate. Drizzle with a little shrimp sauce. Pass remaining sauce. Makes 4 servings.

Company Cauliflower

1 medium head cauliflower, broken
  into flowerets
Salt and pepper
1 cup dairy sour cream
4 ounces sharp process American
  cheese, shredded (1 cup)
2 teaspoons sesame seed, toasted

Cook flowerets, covered, in small amount of boiling salted water till tender, 10 to 15 minutes; drain well. Place *half* the flowerets in a 1-quart casserole. Season with salt and pepper. Spread with *half* the sour cream and *half* the cheese. Top with 1 teaspoon sesame seed. Repeat layers with remaining ingredients.

Bake casserole at 350° till the shredded cheese melts and sour cream is heated through, about 5 minutes. Makes 6 servings.

Cauliflower Scallop

1 10½-ounce can condensed cream
  of celery soup
2 beaten eggs
2 ounces sharp Cheddar cheese,
  shredded (½ cup)
½ cup soft bread crumbs
¼ cup snipped parsley
¼ cup chopped canned pimiento
1 tablespoon instant minced onion
½ teaspoon salt
Dash pepper
2 9-ounce packages frozen
  cauliflower, thawed

Mix together condensed soup, eggs, cheese, bread crumbs, parsley, pimiento, onion, salt, and pepper. Add cauliflower and turn into a 10x6x1½-inch baking dish. Bake at 375° till firm, about 45 minutes. Makes 6 to 8 servings.

Cauliflower with Shrimp Sauce

1 medium head cauliflower, broken
  into flowerets
        . . .
1 10-ounce can frozen condensed
  cream of shrimp soup
½ cup dairy sour cream *or* light
  cream
¼ cup slivered almonds, toasted

Cook flowerets, covered, in small amount of boiling salted water till tender, 10 to 15 minutes; drain cauliflower well.

In a saucepan heat condensed soup over low heat, stirring frequently. Add sour cream *or* light cream; cook and stir just till hot. Add almonds. Pour sauce over hot cauliflowerets. Makes 4 to 6 servings.

CAVIAR *(kav′ ē är′)*—The eggs or roe of several species of sturgeon or similar large fish. Caviar is an expensive delicacy that is usually served as an appetizer.

Sturgeon caviar ranges in color from medium gray to black. Caviar is also prepared from the roe of other fish such as whitefish, carp, and codfish. The roe are green, red, or yellow depending on the fish variety. For example, red caviar is the salted eggs of salmon. Black or gray caviar seems to be the type of caviar chosen by most Americans.

Roe vary in size from a pinhead to a small pea. The larger egg is called "beluga," the name of a white sturgeon from the Black and Caspian Seas. A smaller size is given the name "sevruga," also a variety of sturgeon. Caviar enthusiasts may never agree as to which is better, so let your own taste buds be your flavor guide.

In processing caviar, the roe are first washed and sieved to remove membranes and connective tissue. Next, the eggs are lightly salted and then drained. Finally, the caviar is placed in small jars and processed. Once processed, caviar need not be refrigerated until the jar is opened.

Most sturgeon caviar is imported from Russia and Iran where it is usually sold fresh. Fresh caviar is extremely perishable and must be kept iced. Because its holding time is extremely short, imported fresh caviar is very expensive.

Pressed caviar is from the eggs of immature sturgeon as well as those of advanced maturity. Although usually less expensive than the standard fine-granular caviar, pressed caviar is preferred by some gourmets. It makes a fine canapé spread.

Serve caviar icy cold, but not frozen. You chill it right in a container that is nestled in a bed of crushed ice. Also serve small, thin slices of melba or fresh toast along with a selection of accompaniments such as lemon wedges, finely chopped hard-cooked egg white, sieved hard-cooked egg yolk, minced onion, or snipped chives. Spoon caviar onto the toast, then drizzle with lemon juice and sprinkle with the other accompaniments to suit your taste.

For an unusual flavor, serve a little caviar over broiled fish, or mix it into French or Russian salad dressing for a tossed green salad. The connoisseur of caviar prefers it on toast—"straight"—with no additions. In Russia, caviar is spread on black bread or rolled in tiny, thin buckwheat cakes. These tiny roll-ups are then topped with a dollop of sour cream.

Caviar Appetizers

• Stuff mushroom crowns with caviar.
• Combine cream cheese with red caviar and stuff into celery or artichoke hearts. Or, using a pastry tube, pipe a small amount on crisp rich round crackers.
• Top halved hard-cooked eggs with a tiny amount of caviar and a little minced onion.
• Use as trim for tiny appetizer-size open-face sandwiches.
• Fill miniature cream puffs with caviar.

Trim the top of a folded French omelet with a band of red caviar for a gourmet treat. Sour cream is the accompanying topper.

A simple, yet elegant way to present caviar is nestled in a bed of crushed ice and surrounded with its accompaniments.

Caviar-Stuffed Eggs

    6 hard-cooked eggs
    2 tablespoons butter or margarine
    1 2-ounce jar (3 tablespoons)
        black caviar

Cut eggs in half lengthwise. Carefully remove and sieve egg yolks. Blend in butter or margarine; carefully stir in caviar and dash pepper. Fill egg whites with yolk mixture. Garnish with parsley, if desired. Makes 12 halves.

CAYENNE OR RED PEPPER (kī en', kā-)— A powdery seasoning ground from *Capsicum* pepper pods and seeds. Looking something like paprika, cayenne is not quite as bright in color and is often simply called ground red pepper.

Traditionally there was a difference between cayenne and ground red pepper, cayenne being made from the hottest peppers, while red pepper, not quite as hot, being made from a slightly milder pepper. In the past they were marketed as separate products, but today little distinction is made between the two and many manufacturers even put both names on the label or label the product only red pepper. You can substitute one for the other successfully in most recipes.

The peppers from which cayenne or red pepper is prepared are believed to have had their origin in South America. Today, these peppers are grown in the United States, mainly in Louisiana and South Carolina. They are also imported from Turkey, Japan, Africa, and Mexico.

The process of making cayenne pepper consists of grinding and sifting the dried fruit. Then it is packaged and labeled for the grocery store spice shelf.

Because cayenne is so hot and pungent, use it only in very small amounts to give flavor accent to sauces, cheese or seafood dishes, meat dishes, and eggs. It is also used quite often in both Mexican and Italian dishes. (See also *Spice*.)

CELERIAC (suh ler' ē ak')—A member of the celery family cultivated for its turnip-like root. Other names are celery root, knob celery, and turnip-rooted celery. This low-calorie, winter vegetable is available from October through April.

When shopping for celeriac, choose small-sized roots or knobs since these are best for eating. The large ones tend to be woody and hollow. Because the green top is sparse and inedible, it is usually cut away before the root is marketed. Allow about 1½ pounds for four servings. Store in a cold, moist place.

You must peel the tough outer coat of celeriac before it can be eaten. The peeled root can then be served raw in matchstick strips as an appetizer, or sliced into a salad. If you prefer, it can also be cut up and cooked in water. Dressed with butter or a cream sauce, or mashed, cooked celeriac can be served instead of potatoes on the dinner plate. (See also *Celery*.)

Marinated Celery Root

An unusual vegetable prepared very simply—

Remove and discard green top from 1 medium celery root. Peel root and dice. Cook in boiling water just till tender, about 8 minutes. Drain well. While still warm, cover with French salad dressing. Refrigerate 2 to 3 hours. Serve as an accompaniment with meat or in tomato rosettes as a salad. Makes 4 salad servings.

Shredded carrots add a touch of color and flavor to Celery Slaw. Add this salad to any menu needing something crisp and crunchy.

Celery Root Sauté

    1 medium celery root
    2 tablespoons butter or margarine
    1 tablespoon snipped parsley

Remove and discard green top from the celery root. Peel root and cut into julienne strips. Cook in boiling salted water just till tender, about 8 minutes; drain.

In small saucepan cook butter till brown. Pour over cooked celery root. Season to taste with salt and pepper. Sprinkle with snipped parsley. Makes 4 servings.

CELERY—A vegetable belonging to the parsley family that is eaten raw or cooked.

In early times, wild celery was used for medicinal purposes. Celery still grows wild in some parts of England. It was later domesticated, cultivated, and used as a flavoring agent and a food. The use of celery spread across Europe from Italy to England and France and then to America where commercial growing began in Michigan around the mid-1800's.

Nutritional value: As most dieters know, celery is low in calories. Only about three calories can be counted for a small five-inch inner stalk or 17 calories for one cup diced raw celery. It contains some vitamin A—more in the green varieties than in the yellow type. Celery also contains some of the B vitamins.

Types of celery: Two types of celery are marketed throughout the year. Formerly, yellow celery (which is bleached white) was the most popular, and some are still marketed as stalks or hearts. But preference in recent years has turned to the pascal or green variety with its large and tender stalks. Pascal celery is almost "stringless."

With either type, a bunch is made up of branches or ribs with leaves. These branches surround the heart. Often the word stalk is used for a branch or rib, as well as for a bunch of celery.

How to select: When purchasing celery in the market, look for stalks that are crisp, solid, rigid, and of medium length and thickness. Green leaves that have not been trimmed away should be fresh. Blemishes or decay on outer branches indicate poor quality and the possibility of considerable waste when these outer branches have to be discarded. Avoid bunches of celery with discoloration among the center branches.

How to store: After purchasing celery, rinse the stalk well under cold running water to remove any soil. Enclose tightly

Cheese and celery blend together in Creamy Celery Bake. Pimiento and green pepper bits make this a festive-looking dish.

in foil or clear plastic wrap or place in a plastic bag. Store in the crisper of the refrigerator. Celery will keep from one to two weeks if refrigerated properly.

How to prepare: Separate the branches. Cut off leaves and trim roots. Scrub well. Uncooked chopped celery from 8 branches measures about 2¾ cups.

To cook celery, slice outer branches and cut hearts lengthwise. Cook, covered, in a small amount of boiling salted water till just tender, usually for 10 to 15 minutes.

How to use: Celery can be used many ways. Thoroughly scrubbed and trimmed, it is delicious raw as a relish, salad ingredient, or low-calorie snack. Well-washed celery leaves can add flavor to soups, salads, and stews. Celery can be served cooked as a vegetable dish, cooked in a creamy mixture for soup, or added to recipes when a crisp texture is needed, such as in a stuffing for poultry.

Celery appetizers need a minimum amount of preparation. Cut branches in serving-size lengths, then fill branches with a cheese or peanut butter mixture. Or, cut into sticks or fans and serve as go-alongs with creamy, well-seasoned dips.

Celery Fans

Cut tender celery branches (stalks) in 3- or 4-inch lengths. Make parallel cuts close together from one end *almost* to the other. Or slit both ends almost to the center. (To make fans that curl on top *and* bottom sides, make another cut through strips splitting each in two.) Chill in ice water till strips curl.

Celery Oriental

Slice 6 to 8 large, outside celery branches (stalks) on the bias. Cook in small amount boiling salted water till just crisp-tender; drain.

In saucepan cook 1 cup sliced fresh mushrooms in 3 tablespoons butter or margarine till tender; add celery and ¼ cup toasted blanched almond halves. Toss lightly over low heat just till vegetable mixture is heated through. (Do not overcook.) Makes 4 to 6 servings.

Creamy Celery Bake

A vegetable casserole perfect for company fare—

      4 cups thinly sliced celery
    ¼ cup butter or margarine
      3 tablespoons all-purpose flour
      1 teaspoon salt
      1 cup milk
           • • •
      1 3-ounce can chopped mushrooms, drained (about ½ cup)
      2 tablespoons chopped green pepper
      2 tablespoons chopped canned pimiento
      4 ounces sharp process American cheese, shredded (1 cup)
           • • •
      1 cup soft bread crumbs
      2 tablespoons butter or margarine, melted

In medium skillet cook celery in ¼ cup butter or margarine till tender, about 5 minutes. Push celery to one side; stir in flour and salt. Add milk all at once; cook and stir till mixture thickens and bubbles.

Stir in mushrooms, green pepper, and pimiento. Add cheese and stir till melted. Turn mixture into 10x6x1½-inch baking dish. Combine bread crumbs and the 2 tablespoons melted butter. Sprinkle over casserole. Bake at 350° for 20 minutes. Makes about 8 servings.

Celery Slaw

Goes especially well with poultry or fish—

      1 tablespoon sugar
    ½ teaspoon salt
    ¼ teaspoon paprika
    ⅛ teaspoon pepper
      2 tablespoons salad oil
      1 tablespoon wine vinegar
    ⅓ cup dairy sour cream
           • • •
      3 cups thinly sliced celery
    ½ cup shredded carrot

Combine sugar, salt, paprika, pepper, salad oil, and vinegar. Slowly stir into sour cream. Add to celery and carrot in a bowl. Toss lightly to mix. Makes about 6 servings.

Speedy Celery Stuffing

  1 7- or 8-ounce package herb-
     seasoned stuffing mix
  1 teaspoon ground sage
  1 cup chopped celery
  ½ cup chopped onion
  ¼ cup butter or margarine
  1¼ cups chicken broth

To stuffing mix add sage, celery, and onion. Add butter to chicken broth; heat. Add broth mixture to stuffing. Toss lightly. Use as a stuffing for two 4- to 5-pound chickens or one 10-pound turkey. Makes about 6 cups stuffing.

Cream of Celery Soup

  1½ cups diced celery
  ⅓ cup chopped onion
     • • •
  2 tablespoons butter or margarine
  2 tablespoons all-purpose flour
  ½ teaspoon salt
  3 cups milk
     Butter or margarine

Cook celery and onion, covered, in 1 cup boiling salted water till tender, about 13 minutes.

Meanwhile, prepare white sauce by melting 2 tablespoons butter in saucepan over low heat. Stir in flour, salt, and dash white pepper. Add milk all at once. Cook quickly, stirring constantly till mixture thickens and bubbles. Stir into cooked celery and liquid. Heat through. Season to taste with salt and pepper. Top servings with butter. Makes 6 servings.

Dried celery flakes for use as seasoning are available on the spice and herb shelves in most supermarkets. One tablespoon celery flakes equals two tablespoons fresh chopped celery. (See also *Vegetable*.)

CELERY CABBAGE—Alternate name for Chinese Cabbage. (See also *Chinese Cabbage*.)

CELERY SALT—A blend of table salt and ground celery seed. Used primarily as a seasoning, it is particularly good with poultry, fish, in soups, and mixed with tomato juice as an appetizer. (See also *Salt*.)

Herb Fried Chicken

  ½ teaspoon dried thyme leaves,
     crushed
  ½ teaspoon dried marjoram leaves,
     crushed
  ½ teaspoon celery salt
  1 2½- to 3-pound ready-to-cook
     broiler-fryer chicken, cut up
  ⅓ cup all-purpose flour
  3 tablespoons shortening

Combine thyme, marjoram, celery salt, 1 teaspoon salt, and ¼ teaspoon pepper. Sprinkle over chicken. Roll chicken in flour. Slowly brown chicken pieces in melted shortening, about 15 minutes, being careful not to crowd pieces in skillet. Reduce heat. Cover and cook till tender, 30 to 40 minutes, uncovering skillet last 10 minutes of cooking. Makes 4 servings.

CELERY SEED—The small, olive brown seeds of a wild variety of celery called smallage. The whole seeds lend a celery-like flavor to salad dressings, homemade potato salads, soups, stews, cabbage coleslaws, relishes, and pickles.

Patio Potato Salad

  ⅓ cup sugar
  1 tablespoon cornstarch
  ½ cup milk
  ¼ cup vinegar
  1 egg
  ¼ cup butter or margarine
  ¾ teaspoon celery seed
  ¼ teaspoon dry mustard
  ¼ cup chopped onion
  ¼ cup mayonnaise or salad dressing
  7 medium potatoes, cooked,
     peeled, and diced
  3 hard-cooked eggs, chopped
     Paprika

In saucepan combine sugar and cornstarch; add next 6 ingredients and ¾ teaspoon salt. Cook and stir over low heat till bubbly. Remove from heat; add onion and mayonnaise. Cool. Combine potatoes and hard-cooked eggs; gently fold in dressing. Chill. Just before serving sprinkle with paprika. Makes 6 servings.

CELLOPHANE NOODLES—Very slender, white, translucent, round noodles made from powdered mung beans or pea starch. Dried and sold in skeins, these noodles are used in Chinese cookery. Cellophane noodles, sometimes called bean thread, are available in oriental grocery stores.

The noodles have very little flavor of their own but will absorb the flavor of the broth or liquid in which they are cooked. Another favorite way to use them is as a crisp garnish for stir-fried dishes. The loosened skein of dried noodles is fried quickly in deep fat.

CELLULOSE—A carbohydrate that is the chief material found in the cell walls of plants. In addition to providing the structural framework for all fruits and vegetables, cellulose is present in the shells of legumes and both the outer layer and inner cellwork of cereal grains.

Although not considered digestible except if from young tender produce, cellulose is an important contributor of bulk or roughage to the diet and is necessary to maintain body regularity.

CEPE *(sehp)*—A large, fleshy mushroom found in France. The cap measures six or more inches in diameter and ranges from yellow to reddish brown in color. Its flavor is usually more pronounced than that of American cultivated mushrooms.

CEREAL—1. Edible seed of grains. 2. Grasses that produce the grains. 3. Manufactured products made from grains. Wheat, corn, rice, oats, rye, and barley are the most common cereal grains. Although not cereal grains, buckwheat and soybean products are sometimes used as cereals or blended with cereal mixtures.

The word cereal comes from an ancient Roman festival known as the *Cerealia*. It originated about 500 B.C. and honored Ceres, the goddess of grain. This springtime ceremony sought the goddess's protection for the coming crop.

Grain was not the only food, but it was so basic to life that measures of grain became one of the earliest forms of money. In Mesopotamia, both grain and silver were used as legal tender.

Kernels of different cereal grains will vary in size and shape. However, their basic structure is similar; each contains the bran, the endosperm, and the germ. The thin outer layers, called bran, serve as a protective covering. The tender endosperm which constitutes approximately 85 percent of the kernel, contains the food supply for the growing plant. The third segment is the germ or embryo.

Many of the types of grains you eat today were cultivated in prehistoric times. Stone Age peoples ate roasted grains, and pounded some between stones to make a flour. As long ago as 3000 B.C., rice was grown and used in the Orient, and corn was eaten in the Americas by the Aztecs. While no exact date is recorded, barley and wheat are known to have been cultivated and used long before oats and rye.

By the time of the ancient Egyptians, Greeks, and Romans, grain cultivation was quite highly developed, as was grinding or milling. The Romans developed a mill that could be turned by men or animals, and they, as well as the Egyptians, developed methods for sieving their grains to remove coarse chaff. Later came the use of water wheels and power mills.

Today, much of this work is done by great, modern, electrically powered grain mills with roller-crusher devices and machines for hulling and refining grains.

Nutritional value: Cereal in all its forms plays an important role in man's diet by providing good nutrition at a relatively low cost. Milling and processing affect the amounts of nutrients in the final cereal product purchased by the homemaker. Label information on each package gives details about the specific food.

Whole-grain cereals along with restored or enriched cereals are good sources of iron, phosphorus, and the B vitamins, thiamine and niacin. They are, however, low in vitamin C and, unless enriched, vitamin D also. Only yellow corn contains vitamin A in any significant amount.

In their natural state, cereal grain products provide energy in the form of carbohydrate. Fat is a minor component. Although cereal protein is abundant and economical, it is more useful to the body when combined with other protein sources. Milk, a natural serving partner, is the perfect nutritional complement.

Besides the protein boost, milk supplements the calcium and riboflavin present. When the milk is fortified with vitamins A and D, the nutritional score for the combination is even higher. The nutritional value of milk is enhanced by the partnership, too. Nutrients present in smaller amounts in milk, such as thiamine, niacin, and iron, are present in larger amounts in cereal. This highly nutritious partnership holds true whether the milk used is whole or skim. The only difference is that the milk fat (butterfat) in whole milk will increase the fat content and caloric value of the final serving.

Types of cereal: These nutritionally necessary foods are generally grouped according to whether the cereal is served hot or cold. Farina, oatmeal, whole wheat, rolled wheat cereals and some grain combinations are in the group to be served hot. The cold cereals include precooked crisp flakes, puffs, shredded biscuits of various sizes, and many grain combinations.

Hot cereals require varying amounts of cooking depending on the processing the grains have received. Each cereal product has its own characteristic flavor and texture. For additional variety, maple, malt, or chocolate flavorings may be added to some cereals by processors before being placed on the market.

Cereals labeled quick cooking are processed in thinner, smaller particles that cook more rapidly than the regular version of the grain. Several are marketed in instant form and need only the addition of boiling water to provide a serving of hot, nourishing cereal.

Cold cereals are crisp, ready-to-eat favorites that appear on the breakfast table in a wondrous assortment of shapes and flavors. They are flaked, shredded, puffed, popped, or formed into intriguing shapes designed to delight the youngsters, who consume them in great quantities. Many cereals are presweetened which makes them good snack food as well as breakfast food. Raisins or special flavorings packed with the cereal add to the fun.

How to store: Both dry or uncooked cereals are best stored tightly covered in a cool, dry place. Most ready-to-eat cereals are packaged with an innerlining between carton and food. Care in opening and reclosing both package and lining will help maintain freshness throughout storage.

Generous spoonfuls of melting Honey Butter enhance piping hot bowls of Whole Wheat for breakfast. Pass milk, if desired.

How to use: Breakfast is, by far, the meal at which cereal is most frequently served. The crisp ready-to-eat favorites are poured from the package into a bowl and topped with milk, fruit, and sugar, if desired. Brown sugar, honey, or one of the flavored pancake syrups can be substituted for the sugar as a special treat. Hot cereals take only minutes to prepare and can be dressed up with fruit and syrups in much the same way as their crisp counterparts.

Cereals have many uses as cooking ingredients. Rice and oats can be blended with meat mixtures when preparing loaves and casseroles to help stretch the meat servings and to improve the texture of the finished dish. Crushed flakes may be used in burgers from time to time, but they are at their best as a crusty coating for fish and chicken or as a quick topping for baked main dishes. Barley and rice are favorites in soups or served with creamed foods and in casseroles.

Cereals are no strangers in cookies, desserts, and quick breads where their nut-like crunch adds flavor and texture.

(See *Grain* and individual cereals for additional information.)

Hot Whole Wheat and Honey Butter

   ½ cup butter or margarine
   ¼ cup honey
     Ready-to-cook whole wheat cereal

Prepare Honey Butter by whipping butter till fluffy. Slowly add honey, beating until smooth.

Prepare 4 servings of ready-to-cook whole wheat cereal according to package directions. Spoon into bowls. Top with Honey Butter.

Spicy Raisin Oatmeal

Bring 3½ cups cold water to a brisk boil. Add 1 cup seedless raisins, 1 teaspoon salt, 1 teaspoon ground cinnamon, and ½ teaspoon ground nutmeg. Slowly stir in 1½ cups quick-cooking rolled oats, making sure water continues to boil. Reduce heat; cook 5 minutes, stirring occasionally. Remove from heat; cover oatmeal and let stand 5 minutes. Serve hot with sugar and cream or milk. Makes 4 servings.

Cerealsnaps

Crisp goodies to fill the cookie jar—

   ½ cup butter or margarine
   ½ cup brown sugar
   ½ cup granulated sugar
   1 egg
   1 teaspoon vanilla
  1¼ cups sifted all-purpose flour
   ½ teaspoon baking powder
   ½ teaspoon baking soda
   ½ teaspoon salt
   2 cups crisp rice cereal
   1 3½-ounce can flaked coconut
       (1⅓ cups)

Cream butter with sugars; add egg and vanilla, creaming till fluffy. Sift together dry ingredients; stir into creamed mixture. Stir in cereal and coconut. Shape in ¾-inch balls; place about 2½ inches apart on *ungreased* cookie sheet. Bake at 350° till lightly browned, about 10 minutes. Cool slightly; remove from pan. Cool on rack. Makes 5 dozen cookies.

Crunchy Date Rounds

Sugared flakes add crunch to tender date cookies—

   ½ cup butter or margarine
   ½ cup granulated sugar
   ¼ cup brown sugar
   1 egg
   1 teaspoon vanilla
   1 cup sifted all-purpose flour
   ½ teaspoon baking powder
   ¼ teaspoon baking soda
   ½ teaspoon salt
   ½ cup chopped walnuts
   1 cup snipped pitted dates
  1½ cups presweetened cereal flakes,
       coarsely crushed

Combine butter, sugars, egg, and vanilla; beat well. Sift together flour, baking powder, soda, and salt; gradually add to creamed mixture, blending well. Stir in nuts and dates. Drop from teaspoon into crushed cereal flakes, rolling to coat well. Bake about 2 inches apart on *ungreased* cookie sheet at 375° till top springs back when lightly touched, about 10 to 12 minutes. Makes 3 dozen.

Pass the Scramble at snack time or whenever coffee or iced beverages are served. It is a zippy concoction of mixed nuts, pretzel sticks, and a multitude of crisp ready-to-eat cereals.

Scramble

    2 pounds mixed salted nuts
    1 11-ounce package spoon-size
         shredded-wheat biscuits
    1 10½-ounce package doughnut-
         shaped oat cereal
    1 6-ounce package bite-size
         shredded rice squares
    1 7-ounce package small pretzel
         twists
    1 5¾-ounce package slim
         pretzel sticks
    1 4½-ounce can pretzel bits
    2 cups salad oil
    2 tablespoons Worcestershire sauce
    1 tablespoon garlic salt
    1 teaspoon seasoned salt

Mix first 7 ingredients in large pan or roaster. Combine remaining ingredients; pour over cereal mixture. Bake at 250° for 2 hours, stirring and turning mixture with wooden spoon every 15 minutes (do not crush). Makes 9 quarts.

Berry-Cereal Parfaits

    1 quart vanilla ice cream
    2 10-ounce packages frozen sliced
         strawberries, partially thawed
    2 cups presweetened cornflakes

In each tall parfait glass, layer about ¼ cup ice cream, about 3 tablespoons strawberries, and ¼ cup cornflakes. Top with another ¼ cup ice cream. Garnish with berries. Serves 8.

Easy Italian Chicken

Oven baked with a crispy, garlic-flavored crust—

1 2½- to 3-pound ready-to-cook
   broiler-fryer chicken, cut up
½ cup butter or margarine,
   softened
½ envelope garlic salad dressing
   mix (1 tablespoon)
1 cup cornflake crumbs
   Paprika

Pat chicken pieces dry with paper towels. Thoroughly combine softened butter or margarine and salad dressing mix. Using a spatula, spread butter mixture over chicken pieces. Roll in cornflake crumbs. Sprinkle chicken lightly with paprika.

In a shallow pan arrange chicken pieces skin side up making sure that they do not touch one another. Bake at 375° until tender, about 1 hour. It is not necessary to turn the pieces. Makes 4 servings.

Mock Indian Pudding

Crushed cornflakes replace cornmeal in this version of a traditional New England dessert—

2 slightly beaten eggs
½ cup light molasses
¼ cup sugar
1 tablespoon butter or margarine,
   melted
½ teaspoon ground cinnamon
¼ teaspoon salt
¼ teaspoon ground cloves

. . .

3 cups milk
4 cups cornflakes, coarsely
   crushed
1 pint vanilla ice cream

Combine eggs, molasses, sugar, melted butter, cinnamon, salt, and cloves; mix well. Stir in milk and cornflake crumbs. Pour into greased 1½-quart casserole. Place in shallow pan on oven rack; pour hot water into pan till 1-inch deep. Bake at 350° till knife inserted halfway between center and edge comes out clean, about 1 hour. Serve pudding warm, topped with ice cream. Makes 6 servings.

Peachy Rice Pudding

1 cup uncooked packaged
   precooked rice
1 cup milk
2 tablespoons butter or margarine
1 16-ounce can peach slices,
   undrained
2 beaten eggs
   Dash ground nutmeg

In saucepan combine rice and milk; bring to boiling. Cover; reduce heat and cook 5 minutes. Stir in butter, peaches, eggs, and nutmeg. Cook and stir 2 minutes more. Sprinkle with additional nutmeg. Serve with cream. Serves 4.

Crunch Sticks

1 package refrigerated biscuits
   (10 biscuits)
   Milk
1 cup crisp rice cereal,
   coarsely crushed
1 tablespoon caraway, celery,
   or dillseed

Cut biscuits in half. Roll each piece into 4-inch pencil-like stick. Brush with milk. Mix cereal crumbs, seed, and 1 teaspoon salt in shallow pan (be sure salt is well distributed). Roll sticks in cereal mixture. Place on greased baking sheet; bake at 450° till lightly browned, about 8 to 10 minutes. Makes 20 sticks.

CHAFING DISH—Cooking equipment consisting of a deep metal pan with a handle, a container for water, and a heat source in a frame to support the two pans. The unit may be of modern design and material or of classic silver; in any case, chafing dishes are used at the table to cook foods or to keep them warm.

The cooking pan is called a blazer and the water basin a bain-marie. Together they function as a double boiler for preparing sauces or holding foods at serving temperature. The blazer pan alone can be used like a skillet directly over the heat.

Portable heating equipment, while currently popular, is by no means new. The early Babylonians and Egyptians used braziers as space heaters to take the chill out of a room. Over the centuries the design changed and these little stoves on legs moved from floor to tabletop. Cooking became their chief function. A further improvement occurred when crude versions of the double boiler were used on the little stoves. They were clumsy at first, and it was only natural that a single piece of equipment should evolve.

Over the years chafing dishes became more elegant. For example, silversmiths in Europe and later in colonial America did a good business making chafing dishes for use in the finest homes. Chafing dishes were extremely practical. In large homes the kitchen was often a great distance from the dining area. Foods in chafing dishes could be kept hot in the dining room until everyone was served.

Credit for many of the refinements in the chafing dish and the cookery for which it is used goes to Alexis Soyer, a Frenchman of remarkable talent. He lived in the nineteenth century and built his reputation as chef at the Reform Club, the London headquarters for a gourmet society. He was not only a superb cook, but also an inventor and cook book writer.

Because he delighted in preparing delicate sauces in the same room in which the dishes were served, his adaptations of the burner and his use of the water bath made possible this elegant food.

Chafing dishes have long been considered essential in fine restaurants where cooking spectacular dishes at the diner's own table is a specialty of the house. Now they are becoming popular for home entertaining as well. No matter how simple, chafing-dish food looks glamorous, and the hostess spends less time in the kitchen —more with her guests.

How to use a chafing dish: This versatile piece of equipment fills many serving needs. Sometimes, hot appetizer dips or one-dish meals are completely prepared in the kitchen, then transferred to the chafing dish to keep hot at the table. In this case the water pan is used to distribute the heat evenly over the bottom of the blazer. Egg-yolk sauces and cheese rarebits are also cooked over hot water.

The blazer pan alone lends itself to the preparation of simple food such as scrambled eggs. It is also used for glamorous foods flamed at the table such as Cherries Jubilee, Crepes Suzette, and Steak Diane.

For actual cooking at the table, most hostesses prefer heat that can be adjusted. Chafing dishes are usually equipped with either an alcohol burner or a container for canned heat. The alcohol burner uses denatured alcohol which can be purchased at a hardware store. The burner has a lever or regulator by which the intensity of the flame can be adjusted. On the other hand, when canned heat is used, the holder should have a sliding lid so that the amount of flame exposed can be increased or decreased to suit the food.

Candles, used in some types of food warmers, do not give off enough heat for cooking in a chafing dish.

Table-side cookery should be the spectacular result of careful planning and preparation. The secret is to have everything ready before guests arrive.

Choose speedy recipes for chafing dish cookery. The dish may require several ingredients, but cooking time and cooking

Wreathed in cheese, chopped onion, and olives, a peppy Sombrero Spread awaits the dipping of a crisp tostada or corn chip.

steps at the table should be kept to a minimum. For example, if the sauce for a curry should take more than a few minutes to prepare, make it in advance, pour it into the chafing dish, and add the last few ingredients at the table.

Sometimes it is faster to brown the meat in a skillet on the range in the kitchen, then transfer to the chafing dish for final assembly or cooking at the table. (See *Cherries Jubilee, Crepes, Steak Diane, Stroganoff* for additional information.)

Sombrero Spread

½ pound ground beef
½ cup chopped onion
¼ cup hot-style catsup
½ teaspoon chili powder
½ teaspoon salt
1 8-ounce can undrained red
   kidney beans
2 ounces sharp process American
   cheese, shredded (½ cup)
¼ cup chopped pimiento-stuffed
   green olives
Tostadas

In 8-inch skillet or blazer pan of chafing dish, cook meat and ¼ *cup* of the onion till meat is brown. Stir in catsup, chili powder, and salt. Add beans; mash mixture very well. Heat through. Garnish with cheese, olives, and remaining onion. Place over hot water to keep warm. Serve with tostadas. Makes 2 cups.

Easy Cheese Dunk

½ 10½-ounce can condensed cream
   of mushroom soup
2 6-ounce rolls garlic-flavored
   cheese food, cut up
3 tablespoons dry sherry
1 teaspoon Worcestershire sauce
⅛ to ¼ teaspoon bottled hot
   pepper sauce

In saucepan or blazer pan of chafing dish, combine soup and cheese food. Heat over very low heat till cheese melts, stirring often to blend. Add remaining ingredients. Keep hot for dipping. Makes about 2 cups.

Sweet-and-Sour Surprises

2 tablespoons cornstarch
2 tablespoons sugar
1 chicken bouillon cube, crumbled
1 cup pineapple juice
½ cup water
⅓ cup vinegar
2 tablespoons soy sauce
1 tablespoon butter or margarine
½ pound tiny meatballs, cooked
½ pound shrimp, cooked
½ pound chicken livers, cooked

Combine cornstarch, sugar, and bouillon cube. Add pineapple juice, water, vinegar, soy sauce, and butter or margarine. Cook and stir till thick and bubbly. Cover; simmer 5 minutes longer. Transfer to blazer pan of chafing dish. Group meatballs, shrimp, and livers in sauce. Heat through. Set pan over bain-marie; serve hot with cocktail picks. Makes 1½ cups sauce.

Easy Shrimp Sauté

6 tablespoons butter or margarine
1 clove garlic, minced
1½ pounds shelled raw
   shrimp (3 cups)
¼ cup dry sherry
2 tablespoons snipped parsley
Hot cooked rice

Melt butter in blazer pan of chafing dish or skillet; add garlic and cook slightly. Add shrimp; cook, stirring frequently, till shrimp are tender and turn pink, about 5 minutes. Stir in wine and parsley. Heat to boiling. Serve with rice. Makes 4 to 6 servings.

Beef and Lima Skillet

Cook one 10-ounce package frozen lima beans according to package directions; drain. In skillet or blazer pan of chafing dish brown 1 pound ground beef. Combine ½ clove garlic, minced; 1 tablespoon cornstarch; 1 tablespoon sugar; 2 tablespoons soy sauce; 1 teaspoon prepared horseradish; ½ cup water; and few drops bottled hot pepper sauce. Add to meat. Cook till thick and bubbly. Add limas; cook and stir till heated through. Makes 6 servings.

CHALLAH—The traditional Jewish Sabbath bread or twist. The loaf is leavened with yeast and has a velvety crumb. The dough gets its golden color from the addition of eggs and sometimes saffron. The loaf is usually braided and the top brushed with egg just before baking.

CHAMPAGNE—A sparkling white wine produced in the Champagne region of France, northeast of Paris. High-quality sparkling white and pink champagne wines are also produced in the United States. Vintage champagne, either domestic or imported, is wine that has been made from grapes which were grown all in the same year. Although vineyards and winemaking had been known in France since Roman times, it was a legendary Benedictine monk who in the late 1600's developed a method for capturing the "devil's wine." This was the local name for wine that formed a gas during aging and burst forth from the bottle. Dom Pérignon determined that the sparkle in the bubbly wine was carbon dioxide and devised a way to cork the bottle securely to hold the bubbles in. This knowledgeable man is also credited with establishing methods of mixing or blending wines for highest quality.

How champagne is produced: Climate, variety of grapes, and careful tending of the vine determine the quality of the final wine. The right amount of sun at the right time during the growing season to develop the flavor and sugar content of the grape influences the quality and handling of the wine at every stage of processing. At the right moment of ripeness, the grapes are harvested, and the juice pressed, mixed with the sugar if needed, and allowed to ferment. During fermentation the sugars are changed to alcohol and carbon dioxide is formed. Development of this new wine is carefully watched at each stage. It is bottled in the spring when the right amount of fermentation has been achieved.

Champagne and sparkling wines receive a second fermentation. It is this second process which gives the wine its sparkle. At the time the new wine is bottled, a yeast culture and syrup are added. The wine is allowed to age for three to four years. But it is not forgotten. During these many months the bottles of wine are placed cork-side down in racks and turned gently at regular intervals so that any sediment in the wine will collect and settle at the neck of the bottle.

Finally, it is time to remove the temporary cork along with the collected sediment. The disgorging, as it is called, must be done very rapidly and carefully so that a minimum of wine comes out with the sediment. Over the years several techniques have been used, but today many wine producers accomplish the disgorging by freezing only the neck of the inverted bottle. When the cork is removed, the pressure of the gas inside the wine will push out the frozen sediment.

Any lost wine is quickly replaced with wine from another bottle containing wine from the same year or a blend designed to produce the desired flavor and quality. If sweetness is desired, it is added at this point. Then, the new cork is set firmly down into the bottle. The final step is to wire it tightly into place.

According to the amount of sweetness, the wine will be *brut* (very dry), *extra dry*, or *demi sec* (fairly sweet). When no sweetening is added, the wine is designated *natural: Brut* is the most popular.

In the United States a bulk method for the making of champagne also has been developed. It is a less expensive process and the finished wine is therefore less costly. The second period of fermentation takes place in the closed tank. When the champagne is ready to be bottled, it is filtered and bottled under pressure to preserve the precious bubbles. When champagne is prepared by the bulk process, the label will so state.

How to serve champagne: It is a festive wine served chilled, but not icy cold. There are two satisfactory methods for chilling champagne. You can place the bottle in the refrigerator for about an hour or let it stand about 15 minutes in an ice bucket. Whichever method is chosen, be careful to avoid shaking the bottle.

To remove the cork with a minimum loss of champagne when it "pops," carefully loosen the wire fastener, keeping a thumb over the cork. Rest the bottle on the table while loosening the wire; you'll have better control of the situation.

Then pick up the bottle in one hand and grasp the cork in the other; twist the bottle rather than the cork. There will be a resounding pop when it slips out, but the outpouring wine is easily captured if you keep a wine glass handy.

At one time the shallow saucer champagne glass—with or without a hollow stem—was prized for serving champagne. Now the eight-ounce tulip-shaped glass is a popular choice, but the all-purpose wine glass will do nicely, too.

Because of its sparkle, and its reputation as a beverage for celebrations, champagne is often used in punch or cocktails at receptions. Many hostesses enjoy serving champagne when entertaining at brunch. (See also *Wines and Spirits*.)

Orange Champagne Cocktail

1 4/5 pint bottle (1¾ cups)
    champagne, chilled
2 7-ounce bottles ginger ale,
    chilled (about 2 cups)
1 cup orange juice, chilled
    Fresh strawberries, washed,
    hulled, and sliced

Combine beverages in pitcher. Serve in glasses with a few strawberry slices. Serves 6 to 8.

Cold Duck

For each serving, combine one part chilled champagne and one part chilled sparkling burgundy in a champagne glass.

CHAMPIGNON   *(sham pin' yuhn)* — The French word for mushroom, particularly edible field varieties.

CHAPATI *(cuh pa' tē)*—The handmade flat bread of India prepared from whole wheat flour and water. The unleavened dough is first patted into a paper-thin, flat pancake which resembles the Mexican tortilla and then it is baked on a hot griddle.

Chapati

2 cups sifted all-purpose flour
¼ cup salad oil
7 tablespoons water

Sift together flour and 1 teaspoon salt. Add oil, mixing well with hands. (Dough will be very stiff.) Knead 5 to 7 minutes till dough has satiny appearance. Pinch off pieces of dough about 1½ inches in diameter. Roll each to 6-inch circle. Brown on both sides on lightly greased hot griddle. Dot with butter or margarine, if desired. Makes about 1 dozen.

CHANUKAH—Hanukkah, the Jewish Festival of Lights celebrated late in December. (See also *Hanukkah*.)

CHAPON—A crusty piece of French bread well rubbed with a cut clove of garlic, then tossed with salad greens. The chapon is discarded before the salad is served. Thus, you add the flavor of garlic without adding pieces of garlic. Chapon is also the French word designating a capon.

Chapaties, lightly browned and hot from the griddle, are traditional accompaniments for the pungent curries served in India.

CHARCOAL—A black substance obtained by heating or partially burning organic matter. This organic matter can be certain animal or vegetable substances such as bones or, most often, wood. Large pieces smolder in the presence of little air so the volatile matter is removed. This produces an impure carbon product which is porous and lightweight.

Charcoal has a number of properties that are used in the manufacture or preparation of foods. It removes coloring from liquids, absorbs gases, and gives off intense heat when burned.

Charcoal is used as a purifying agent, both commercially and in the home. As a commercial agent, it is used to filter out the color in wines and liqueurs, to decolorize beet-sugar juices, and to purify water and absorb odors if present. In the house, homemakers can place lumps of charcoal in the refrigerator to absorb any unpleasant odors.

Charcoal is best known and most often used in the home as a fuel for barbecuing foods. It produces a cleaner, more intense heat than wood does, and it is compact, lightweight, and easy to store.

Either briquets or lumps are used in barbecuing. Briquets are made from ground charcoal which is pressed into uniform blocks. Because of their uniformity, briquets provide more even heat. Lumps ignite and are ready for cooking faster, but they burn out faster than briquets.

Briquets and lumps are sold in 5-, 10-, 20-, and 40-pound sacks. Some have a self-starting feature, and some add a hickory or other special flavor to the food.

Store charcoal in a dry place to protect it from the moisture in the air. And be sure you are using it in a well-ventilated area, for burning charcoal gives off carbon monoxide. Start the fire with an electric starter if one is available and an outlet is nearby. Or, use liquid lighter. Just sprinkle it on the charcoal slowly, giving it a chance to be absorbed. After a few minutes, light the briquets with a match in several places. (Never use kerosene or gasoline in place of the liquid lighter as they are dangerous.) Once the charcoal is burning it will take about 45 minutes longer to reach the correct cooking temperature.

Self-starting charcoal is lighted simply by putting a match to it. Charcoal can be used a second time if allowed to dry thoroughly after the fire has been smothered or doused. (See also *Barbecue*.)

CHARD—A variety of the beet, also called Swiss chard. Its large green leaves and white, succulent stalks have a mild flavor reminiscent of asparagus. The root is not used in cooking.

Chard is a rich source of vitamin A; it has some vitamin C, iron, and B vitamins. A serving averages 20 calories.

This vegetable is most likely to be found in the markets during summer and fall months, though it's not commonly stocked. Those who are especially fond of chard can easily grow it in home gardens.

When selecting chard, choose tender, green leaves and crisp stalks. One pound makes two servings. Store in crisper of the refrigerator and use within two days.

To prepare chard, wash it several times and cut into pieces. Boil till tender, about 10 to 20 minutes; drain and season. Salt and pepper, butter, and lemon juice are good flavor accents. The stalk can also be sautéed. Leaves can be cooked like spinach or used in soups. (See also *Vegetable*.)

CHARLOTTE (*shär' luht*)—A dessert with a sweet filling surrounded by cake or bread. The typical charlotte is made in a mold lined with cake or thin, crisp bread and filled with a fruit, whipped cream, or custard mixture. It is usually served cold, although the oldest variety, apple charlotte, is served hot. (See also *Dessert*.)

CHARLOTTE RUSSE (*shär luht r̄oos'*)—A well-chilled charlotte made with sponge cake or ladyfingers and filled with any flavor of Bavarian cream.

The creation of this dessert is credited to Carême (1783-1833), the illustrious French cook. He first made it for high-ranking Frenchmen and foreign dignitaries. The name was charlotte parisienne originally. Later it became known as charlotte russe in honor of Czar Alexander I.

In the 1920's this dessert gained in popularity. The charlotte russe became much easier to mold and keep well chilled with the introduction of the refrigerators in the home. Convenience products have made the charlotte even easier to prepare today. You needn't bake the sponge cake or ladyfingers—buy them. Instead of making Bavarian cream, choose from a wide variety of pudding mixes for a quick filling.

This elegant dessert deserves decorations of whipped cream, fresh fruit, glacé fruit, or even candied flowers.

Serve it any time of the day. Dessert is always special when it's charlotte russe with coffee or tea. (See also *Dessert.*)

Chocolate Charlotte Russe

      1 4½- or 5-ounce package *regular*
            vanilla pudding mix
      1 teaspoon unflavored gelatin
      2 cups milk
      1 4-ounce bar sweet baking
            chocolate
   1½ cups whipping cream
      2 3-ounce packages
            ladyfingers, split

In saucepan combine pudding mix and gelatin; stir in milk. Cook and stir over medium heat till mixture boils. Remove from heat. Break choc-

Line dish generously with waxed paper, so charlotte russe can be lifted out easily without disturbing the frame of ladyfingers.

olate into squares and add to hot pudding mixture. Stir till chocolate is melted. Cool completely; then beat till pudding is smooth.

Whip cream; reserve 1 cup of whipped cream for garnish. Fold remainder into pudding. Line an 8½x4½x2½-inch loaf dish with waxed paper, extending paper beyond rim. Line bottom and sides with ladyfinger halves. Pour in half of the chocolate mixture. Add a layer of ladyfinger halves and the remaining pudding. Top with remaining ladyfinger halves.

Chill 3 to 4 hours or till firm. Lifting the waxed paper, remove charlotte russe from loaf dish and carefully transfer to serving plate; remove waxed paper. Garnish with the reserved whipped cream. Makes 6 servings.

CHARTREUSE—1. An aromatic liqueur. 2. An elaborate molded entrée.

The liqueur was first made in 1607 by Carthusian monks at Grenoble, France. The monks established another distillery in Tarragona, Spain, in 1903 when they were expelled from France.

The formula is still a secret. It is made on a brandy base with spices and herbs, including cinnamon, hyssop, and saffron. There are two types of chartreuse. One is a clear, light green color with a high alcoholic content. The other is yellow with a sweeter, less potent flavor.

Chartreuse can also refer to a molded entrée. This dish was originally made of root vegetables arranged in orderly rows, but later, meat, game, and poultry were included as ingredients. (See also *Liqueur.*)

CHASSEUR (*ṣha sûr'*)—A method of preparing food characterized by the addition of mushrooms as an ingredient or as a garnish. This method is sometimes used with small cuts of meat, poultry, or eggs. A sauce made in the chasseur manner is seasoned with wine and shallots. This may be called a hunter or chasseur sauce.

Glamorous classic made from a mix

Garnish Chocolate Charlotte Russe with → bunches of seedless, green grapes or whipped cream posies topped with candied cherries.

Arrange turkey slices filled with deviled ham in partially set consommé, then cover with more consommé, and chill until firm.

Cut serving of Chaud-Froid of Turkey using a 30-ounce size can with both ends removed. Bend can into oval for an interesting shape.

CHÂTEAUBRIAND *(shä tō brē än')*—A very thick, center cut from the beef tenderloin which is broiled or grilled. This classic was created by Montmireil, chef to French author and statesman, Châteaubriand.

Châteaubriand is usually served with a Béarnaise or château sauce. In restaurants, the menu generally lists it "for two."

Châteaubriand

    1 1½- to 2-pound center-cut beef
         tenderloin
    2 tablespoons butter, melted
       Salt
       Béarnaise Sauce (See *Béarnaise*)

Place meat on rack of broiler pan. Brush with butter. Broil 4 inches from heat, 12 to 15 minutes; season with salt. Turn; brush again. Broil 12 to 15 minutes more; season second side. Outside will be browned and inside will be rare. Serve with Bearnaise Sauce. Serves 2.

CHAUD-FROID *(shō fräw')*—A dish consisting of poultry or game coated with aspic, jelly, or a sauce stiffened with gelatin. Sometimes meat, fish, seafood, tongue, or ham are substituted for the poultry. The translation from French means hot-cold, for the food is prepared hot and eaten cold.

Because of the advance preparation, decorative appearance, and ease in serving, chaud-froid is elegant for buffets.

Chaud-Froid of Turkey

    12 thin slices from cooked boneless
          turkey roast
     2 4½-ounce cans deviled ham
     ½ cup finely chopped celery
     2 tablespoons finely chopped
          dill pickle
     4 teaspoons prepared horseradish
     2 envelopes (2 tablespoons)
          unflavored gelatin
     2 10½-ounce cans condensed
          consommé (gelatin added)
     2 chicken bouillon cubes
        Dash salt

If turkey slices are irregular in shape, trim to an oval about 3 inches at longest point. Mix deviled ham with celery, pickle, and horseradish; spread over 6 turkey slices. Top with remaining turkey slices making 6 "sandwiches."

Soften gelatin in 1 *can* consommé. Combine in a saucepan 2 cups water, bouillon cubes, and softened gelatin mixture; stir over low heat till bouillon and gelatin are dissolved. Add remaining consommé, dash salt, and 2 soup cans cold water. Chill till partially set.

Pour a little *more than half* of the partially set gelatin into 13x9x2-inch baking dish. Arrange the turkey sandwiches in the gelatin. Carefully pour remaining gelatin over sandwiches. Chill till firm. To serve, cut around turkey sandwiches, leaving a narrow border of gelatin on each. Garnish with ripe olives, deviled eggs, and lemon, if desired. Makes 6 servings.

CHAYOTE *(chī ō' tē)*—A green or white fur-rowed vegetable of the squash family. The pear-shaped chayote measures about three inches by eight inches and grows on a vine. Its soft seed is surrounded by a crys-talline-textured flesh. The flavor is rather bland, resembling a cross between cucumber and zucchini. It is low in starch: about 30 calories per serving.

Chayote grows in tropical America, California and the southern United States. The Aztecs and Mayas were eating it before the Spaniards arrived in America.

When buying chayote, choose firm, young vegetables, avoiding any that are soft or wrinkled. Store in the refrigerator until ready to use. Cook as you would summer squash: steam, boil, fry, bake, or mix with other vegetables. Chayote holds its shape in cooking and is suitable for stuffing with meat mixtures. (See also *Squash*.)

CHECKERBERRY — The red fruit of the American wintergreen. It's also called winterberry. Checkerberries are used like cranberries in sauces, pies, puddings, or stuffings. (See also *Wintergreen*.)

CHEDDAR—A firm, ripened, natural cheese. The color ranges from white to a deep yellow. Flavor is rich and nutty.

Cheddar is named for the English village, Cheddar in Somersetshire, where it was first made during the sixteenth century or even earlier. The English brought their skill in making Cheddar to the American colonies where homemakers made it until commercial manufacturing took over the major part of the production.

How Cheddar is produced: Whole milk from cows is used to make Cheddar. Federal law requires that cheese made with raw milk must be aged at least 60 days. Because Cheddar is aged six months to two years, raw or pasteurized milk can be used.

Ironically, the law prohibits importing Cheddar from its place of origin, England. Most Cheddar sold in America comes from New York, Wisconsin, and Vermont.

Nutritional value: Cheddar supplies protein, fat, and minerals. One ounce of the cheese averages about 112 calories.

Types of Cheddar: This popular cheese comes in a variety of flavors to please any taste. The natural unprocessed cheese ranges from very mild to very sharp while the pasteurized processed products are uniformly mild. Coon cheese is a well-cured Cheddar, and Colby is a soft, mild type of Cheddar. Monterey (or Jack) is a related type of semi-soft, ripened cheese.

How to buy: In some stores, Cheddar is cut to order from a block. In this case, select cheese with a good bouquet, smooth texture, and a minimum of holes. Taste, if possible, to determine quality.

Most supermarkets stock prepackaged cheese cut in blocks or wedges, sliced, and shredded. It's impossible to see and taste this cheese before purchase. Experiment with brands and degrees of sharpness to find a personal favorite.

Peak-quality cheese will be selected from those aged from six to fourteen months. Good flavor is not bitter or soapy, and texture should be waxy, not rubbery.

How to store: Cheddar should be stored in the refrigerator in its original wrapper. Once opened, cover with foil or clear plastic wrap to preserve its quality.

How to use: A versatile cheese, Cheddar is eaten plain or used in many recipes. When served plain, it should be at room temperature. The sharp flavor and smooth texture complement fruit and crackers.

Cheddar may appear in any course at mealtime: it might be a main dish or sauce, or perhaps it could be a flavor accent to another food. (See also *Cheese*.)

Firm, tangy Cheddar is all-purpose.

CHEESE

A look at the development of cheese—natural and process—and its role in today's diet.

Cheese is one of the oldest foods and one of the most nutritious foods known to man. An ancient legend credits the discovery of cheese to an Arab who was journeying across the desert, carrying his milk supply in a pouch made from a sheep's stomach. After many hours of travel, he stopped to satisfy his thirst. He found only a thin, watery liquid—most of the milk in the pouch had changed to a solid. Because of an intense hunger and thirst, he tasted the thick, white curd and found it delicious.

The change in the milk—magic to the Arab—is easily explained today. The combined action of the sun's heat and the sheep-stomach enzymes acting on the milk produced a curd. This reaction is used today as a basis for making cheese.

Historians won't hazard a guess about the discoverer of cheese, but they do believe it was developed shortly after the domestication of the cow, around 9000 B.C. One of the earliest written references to cheese occurs in the *Holy Bible,* when David is credited with having carried ten cheeses to Saul's camp at the time he encountered Goliath.

The ancient Greeks praised it as a gift from the God Aristaeus, protector of farmers and shepherds. They fed it to athletes who took part in the Olympic games. They also used cheese to reward children.

Cheese played such an important role in the Roman diet that special kitchens were built by the rich for making cheese. The lower classes had to cure their cheese in public smokehouses. The growth of the Roman empire spread the art of cheesemaking over the continent.

During the Middle Ages, monks in European monasteries began making and improving the existing kinds of cheese. They developed more elaborate and complicated varieties, among them the soft-ripening cheeses for which France is famous. Their work was a turning point in the development of the art of cheesemaking.

Despite the wide popularity which accompanied the development of cheese, its acceptance declined during the Renaissance. Physicians wrote treatises denigrating its value; others attributed strange and suspicious powers to this once popular food. Superstitions linking eating cheese with illness were prevalent during the sixteenth and seventeenth centuries. During the eighteenth century, cheese was once again accepted—rising in popularity almost as quickly as it had fallen.

Fortunately for the New World, cheese accompanied the Pilgrims who settled in America, and with the arrival of cows from Europe, cheesemaking began. Prior to 1850, cheese production was entirely a home dairy operation. The first cheesemaking factory was built in Rome, New York, in 1851. Cheddar cheese was produced from milk supplied by nearby dairy farms. The development of other cheese factories soon spread along the eastern seaboard and westward to Wisconsin. Today, cheese is produced commercially in nearly every state, with Wisconsin and New York leading the nation's production.

The name of a cheese is often a clue to its history. Cheeses from Norway and Sweden often end with "ost," such as Gjetost and Kuminost. The more popular Danish

Quick lunch for a blustery day

← Toasted Cheese Rolls are made with unsliced sandwich loaf and tangy cheese spread. Serve with hot cream of tomato soup.

cheeses have a common suffix, "bo," as in Molbo and Maribo. Many cheeses take their names from the town or area where they originated: Cheddar is an English village, Roquefort is a specific area in France, there's a Camembert in Normandy, Emmenthal or Emmenthaler (Swiss cheese) gets its name from the Emme valley in Switzerland, Parmesan is named for Parma in Italy, and Limburger comes from Limburg in Belgium.

Cheeses developed by the monks were often named after a saint, such as St. Claude and St. Benoit. Some cheeses are named for their appearance or the manner in which they are shaped. The rind of Pineapple cheese resembles the fruit. Brick cheese was originally formed with bricks, just as hand cheese was shaped by hand. Also, a cheese may be named for an ingredient, for example, sage cheese.

How cheese is made: Although cow's milk is most often used in making cheese, milk from sheep, goats, buffalo, camels, reindeer, and other animals is used in other parts of the world. Cheesemaking involves separating milk into its liquid and solid components. This separation is achieved by adding either rennet (made from rennin, an enzyme found in the lining of a calf's stomach) or a special bacterial culture called a "starter."

Either rennet or starter, when added to milk, causes the milk to separate into white, soft lumps known as curd, and a thin, watery liquid called whey.

Different cultures and processes may affect the formation of the curd which, in turn, produces the differences found among the many varieties of cheese. A variation in temperature, moisture, or acidity influences the character of cheese.

After the curd is formed, it is cut or broken into smaller pieces. It may be cut into small cubes, or a special instrument called a cheese harp may be used to "comb" it into very long, thin strips. Once the curd is cut, it is drained to remove the whey, although for some cheeses the draining process is very slight.

Depending upon the cheese being produced, the curd may or may not be salted and pressed. Mold-ripened cheeses are either sprayed on the surface with mold, or they are inoculated with a mold culture to permit mold development throughout the cheese. Some cheeses are ripened under warm, moist conditions; others are ripened in cool, dry rooms. The rotation of the cheese during ripening and the length of time allowed for ripening also influence the texture of the cheese. Thus, at each step of the cheesemaking operation, a slight change in procedure is responsible for producing a different cheese.

Many kinds of cheese acquire their distinctive quality from a flavor additive. The type of mold used determines the characteristic flavors of Roquefort, Gorgonzola, Stilton, and Camembert. Hops are used to flavor German Hop cheese, while clover is used to make Sapsago. Some cheeses are wrapped in grape, fig, or chestnut leaves to absorb these delicate flavors as they ripen. Other cheeses are flavored with caraway seed, grape seed, saffron, hot peppers, cloves, or anise.

Nutritional value: Approximately five quarts of milk are required to make one pound of Cheddar. Thus, Cheddar is a much more concentrated food. The protein content of cheese is about eight times greater than that found in an equal amount of milk; the fat content is about 20 to 30 percent of the total cheese weight.

The number of calories in different types of cheeses varies, but the most popular varieties in the United States market are whole milk cheeses which are very similar in fat and calorie content. In general, one ounce of cheese supplies about 100 calories. In addition, many of the vitamins and minerals normally found in milk—calcium, phosphorus, vitamin A—are present in cheese.

Natural cheese

Cheese made directly from the curd of milk and not reprocessed or blended is known as natural cheese. Many of the natural cheeses are produced from unpasteurized milk. Cheeses are either unripened (uncured or fresh) or ripened (cured). Uncured or unripened cheeses include the normally quite bland cottage and cream

KNOW YOUR CHEESE

1 Provolone (salami-style)
2 Longhorn
3 Midget Cheddar (sharp)
4 Gorgonzola
5 Parmesan
6 Edam
7 Cheddar (sharp)
8 Cheddar (soft)
9 Port du Salut
10 Provolone
11 Smoked Swiss
12 Cheddar (medium-sharp)
13 Swiss
14 Roquefort
15 Cheshire

16 Sapsago
17 Stilton
18 Gourmandise
19 Sharp Cheddar spread
20 Cheddar (sliced)
21 Pimiento cream-cheese dip
22 Bel Paese
23 Grape cheese
24 Bondost
25 Bondost with caraway
   seed
26 Christian IX (Danish
   spiced)
27 Herkimer (a cheddar type)
28 Sage

cheeses. Cured or ripened cheeses range in flavor from the mild Cheddar to the more pungent Limburger. If ripened, enzymes and microorganisms have been allowed to develop the flavor and texture characteristic of the particular kind of cheese. Length of ripening is often indicated on the package label as "mild," "mellow," "medium," "sharp," or "aged."

Classification of natural cheese

The texture of different varieties of natural cheese is classified according to the manner in which it is ripened. In general, the softer the texture, the shorter the ripening period and the higher the moisture content. The blue-vein varieties are ripened with a mold culture which grows throughout the cheese, producing a characteristic flavor and appearance of the specific variety.

Unripened

Soft	Cottage, Cream, Neufchatel, Ricotta	
Firm	Gjetost, Mysost, Mozzarella	

Ripened

Soft	Brie, Camembert, Limburger	
Semisoft	Bel Paese, Brick, Muenster, Port du Salut	
Firm	Cheddar, Colby, Edam, Gouda, Provolone, Swiss	
Very hard	Parmesan, Romano, Sapsago	
Blue-vein	Blue, Gorgonzola, Roquefort, Stilton	

A barbecue bonanza

← Grill-cooked vegetables such as Cheese-Topped Tomatoes and frozen broccoli spears add a fresh flavor to outdoor barbecuing.

Whey, which contains only a small amount of milk fat, is important in producing certain types of cheese. Mysost, Primost, and Gjetost, popular in Scandinavia, are examples of whey cheeses.

How to select natural cheese: Domestic as well as imported cheeses are available in many American markets. However, many imported cheeses have been modified in production to comply with United States standards for cheese. Thus, many of the traditional cheeses made in Europe are available only for local consumption and cannot be imported into the United States.

The largest selection of cheeses is found generally in grocery store dairy counters, foreign food specialty stores, and cheese specialty stores. A cheese is best evaluated by its appearance, feel, smell, and taste. Many retailers offer samples to aid in selection. Knowing the characteristics of a particular variety is helpful.

Many natural cheeses are marketed in the shape unique to that kind: Gouda and Edam, for instance, are always flattened balls; other cheese varieties are characteristically sold in small blocks, wedges, or rounds. Oftentimes in specialty stores, a specific weight of cheese may be ordered, whereas in most local markets, much of the cheese is prepackaged.

How to store natural cheese: The storage quality of cheese varies greatly. In general, the lower the moisture content the longer it may be stored. As a result, firm or very hard, ripened cheeses are less perishable than soft-ripened varieties.

Although the European connoisseur prefers a cool corner for storing cheese, the refrigerator provides the safest storage. Exposure to warm temperatures may cause cheese to "sweat" fat. Cheese should neither lose nor gain moisture—keep it well wrapped. Store blue-vein cheeses in a covered glass dish that allows air around the cheese, but not enough to dry it.

Some cheeses may be frozen although there is usually some loss of texture. To freeze, wrap pieces one-half pound or less in moisture-vaporproof wrap. Freeze cheese quickly at 0° or lower. To use, thaw in refrigerator in unopened package and serve as soon as possible after thawing. Cheeses that may be frozen include Brick, Camembert, Cheddar, Edam, Liederkranz, Mozzarella, Muenster, Parmesan, Port du Salut, Provolone, Romano, and Swiss. Soft cheeses are not recommended for freezing as they tend to separate after thawing.

How to use natural cheese: For best flavor, most cheeses should be served slightly cooler than room temperature, so remove from refrigerator about one hour before serving. Remove soft cheeses, such as Camembert and Limburger, several hours before serving since they should be creamy when eaten. Serve fresh cheeses—cream, cottage, and Neufchatel—chilled.

Occasionally mold may appear on the outside of the cheese during storage in the refrigerator. This mold is not harmful. Simply cut it away and enjoy your cheese.

Natural cheeses are delicious as an appetizer, snack, sandwich, dessert, or as a part of the main dish. Fondue offers an excellent opportunity for serving cheese as a main dish. Try the dessert cheeses with wine and/or fresh fruit. Individual preference generally decides which cheese is served when. But there are over 400 varieties of cheese with which to experiment. Be adventurous and you'll enhance your cheese-eating pleasures.

Cheddar, Swiss, Gruyère, and Parmesan are often used in cooking. Be careful of too-high temperatures and prolonged cooking which causes natural-type cheeses to become leathery and stringy. Cheese requires no further cooking once it is melted. When possible, it should be added near the end of the cooking period. If shredded, grated, or cubed, less time is needed for melting the cheese.

Process cheese

Much of the cheese manufactured and sold in the United States is pasteurized process cheese which is made from natural cheeses. Such cheeses include process cheese food, process cheese spread, cold-pack cheese, and cold-pack cheese food.

Process cheese—It is prepared by grinding and mixing together one or more natural cheeses with the aid of heat and an emulsifying agent. After blending and heating the cheeses, the mixture is poured into moisture-vaporproof containers. Pasteurization halts the action of enzymes and microorganisms; thus, no further ripening occurs. The emulsifier prevents fat separation during processing and helps produce an easy-to-slice cheese which melts readily when heated. The flavor of process cheese depends largely upon the natural cheese used. Pimientos, fruits, nuts, vegetables, meats, or smoke flavor may be added. Process cheese is packed in slices, loaves, and cut portions.

Process cheese food—while it is similar to process cheese, it is higher in moisture and slightly lower in milk fat content. It is prepared with less cheese and has milk, skim milk, or whey solids added. Pimientos, fruits, vegetables, bacon, or smoke flavor may be mixed in with the cheese. Milder in flavor, cheese food melts quicker than process cheese and is often used as a sandwich spread. It is available on the market in slices, rolls, links, and loaves.

Process cheese spread—it has more moisture and less milk fat than process cheese food. It is even easier to spread than cheese food and may contain the same flavoring ingredients as does process cheese. Process cheese spread is available packaged in jars or small loaves.

Cold-pack cheese—it is prepared by grinding and blending natural cheeses which have been well aged. Its flavor is similar to the natural cheeses used, and it is available in jars, rolls, and links.

Cold-pack cheese food—it differs from cold-pack cheese in that it includes skim milk or whey solids. Sweetening agents such as sugar and corn syrup may be added. Cold-pack cheese food may have a smoked flavor and/or contain pimientos, fruits, vegetables, and meats. It is higher in moisture than cold-pack cheese; thus, it is more easily spread. It is found in the local market in jars, rolls, and links.

How to select process cheese: Reading the package label is of utmost importance when purchasing process cheese because of the wide variety of cheeses. The labels on pasteurized process cheese, cheese food, cheese spread, cold-pack cheese (sometimes called Club or Comminuted cheese), and cold-pack cheese food list the varieties of natural cheese used in making the product. Also listed are ingredients that have been added, as in the making of cheese food or cheese spread. Likewise, if a sharp or aged cheese is used, this is indicated.

How to store process cheese: Like natural cheese, process cheese should be stored in the refrigerator. It has a high moisture content and must be wrapped tightly in moisture-vaporproof wrap to prevent drying on the surface of the cheese.

How to use process cheese: Much of the popularity of process cheese is attributed to its relatively mild flavor and ease of use in cooking. For those who object to the more strongly flavored natural cheeses, process cheese offers many of the same flavors in a much milder form. The most popular process cheese, American, is made from natural Cheddar blended with similar varieties. Other process cheeses are made from Brick, Camembert, Gruyère, Limburger, and Swiss.

Unlike natural cheese, process cheese is not likely to string, to become rubbery, or to develop a grainy texture when heated. However, just as with natural cheese, low

To melt natural cheese, add to sauce over hot water. (Use water bath with chafing dish or double boiler.) Stir till melted.

temperatures and short-time cooking are recommended. A versatile food, process cheese lends itself to appetizers, snacks, sandwiches, fondues, and main dishes.

Cheese Sauce

> 2 tablespoons butter or margarine
> 2 tablespoons all-purpose flour
> ¼ teaspoon salt
> 1 cup milk
> 4 ounces sharp natural Cheddar cheese, shredded (1 cup)

In saucepan melt butter; blend in flour and salt. Add milk, stirring constantly, till mixture thickens and bubbles. Remove from heat; add cheese. Stir to melt. Makes 1½ cups.

Swiss-Cheddar Sauce: Prepare Cheese Sauce *except* use 2 ounces sharp natural Cheddar cheese, shredded (½ cup) and 2 ounces Swiss cheese, shredded (½ cup). Makes 1½ cups.

Blue Cheese Sauce: Prepare Cheese Sauce *except substitute* 1 chicken bouillon cube, crumbled, for salt. *Omit* Cheddar cheese; add ¼ cup dairy sour cream and 1 ounce blue cheese, crumbled (¼ cup). Stir to melt. Heat through, *but do not boil.* Makes 1¼ cups.

Swiss Cheese Sauce

> 2 ounces process Swiss cheese, shredded (½ cup)
> ¼ cup mayonnaise or salad dressing
> ½ cup dairy sour cream
> Paprika

Combine cheese and mayonnaise. Cook over low heat, stirring constantly, till cheese melts. (If necessary, beat smooth with rotary beater.) Mix in sour cream; heat through *but do not boil.* Dash with paprika. Serve with hot cauliflower or cooked asparagus spears. Makes 1 cup.

Jiffy Cheese Sauce

Combine one 10½-ounce can condensed cream of mushroom soup with ⅓ cup milk; heat. Add 4 ounces sharp process American cheese, shredded (1 cup). Stir to melt. Makes about 2½ cups.

Rosy Cheese Fondue

>   8 ounces sharp process American
>   cheese, shredded (2 cups)
>   2 ounces blue cheese, crumbled
>   (½ cup)
>   ½ cup condensed cream of tomato
>   soup
>   1 teaspoon Worcestershire sauce
>   2 tablespoons dry sherry
>   Toasted French bread cubes

In heavy saucepan combine first 4 ingredients. Cook and stir over low heat till smooth. Stir in wine. Transfer to fondue pot. Spear bread with fondue fork; dip in fondue. Makes 1 cup.

Creamy Macaroni and Cheese Bake

Cook 2 cups elbow macaroni according to package directions; drain. Combine with ⅓ cup mayonnaise or salad dressing, ¼ cup chopped canned pimiento, ¼ cup chopped green pepper, and ¼ cup finely chopped onion.

Blend together one 10½-ounce can condensed cream of mushroom soup, ½ cup milk, and 2 ounces sharp process American cheese, shredded (½ cup). Stir into macaroni; place in 1½-quart casserole. Top with additional 2 ounces sharp process American cheese, shredded (½ cup). Bake, uncovered, at 400° for 20 to 25 minutes. Makes 4 to 6 servings.

To melt process cheese, slice cheese directly into hot or cold sauce. Heat sauce only till cheese melts, stirring frequently.

Cheese Soufflé

>   ¼ cup butter or margarine
>   ¼ cup all-purpose flour
>   ½ teaspoon salt
>   Dash cayenne
>   1 cup milk
>   8 ounces sharp process
>   American cheese, thinly sliced
>   4 eggs, separated

Melt butter; blend in flour, salt, and cayenne. Add milk all at once; cook over medium heat, stirring constantly, till mixture thickens and bubbles. Remove sauce from heat. Add thinly sliced cheese; stir till cheese melts.

Beat egg yolks till very thick and lemon-colored. *Slowly* add cheese mixture, stirring constantly; cool slightly. Beat egg whites to stiff peaks. Gradually pour yolk mixture over egg whites; fold together. Pour into *ungreased* 1½-quart soufflé dish or casserole.

For a top hat that puffs in the oven, trace a circle with spoon through mixture 1 inch from edge and 1 inch deep. Bake at 300° for 1¼ hours or till knife inserted off-center comes out clean. Immediately break apart into servings with 2 forks. Makes 4 servings.

Cheese Ramekins

>   3 ounces sharp process American
>   cheese, shredded (¾ cup)
>   2 slightly beaten egg yolks
>   1 cup soft bread crumbs
>   1 cup milk, scalded
>   2 stiffly beaten egg whites

Reserve 2 tablespoons of the cheese. Combine remaining cheese, egg yolks, bread crumbs, and hot milk. Fold in egg whites. Turn into two 1½-cup casseroles. Top with reserved cheese. Bake at 325° for 35 to 40 minutes, or till knife inserted just off-center comes out clean. Serve immediately. Makes 2 servings.

Light as a feather

Puffy Cheese Soufflé billows with top-hat →
appearance as it bakes in the oven. Delicate cheese flavor makes this a memorable dish.

Toasted Cheese Rolls

Cut crusts from top and sides of 1 unsliced sandwich loaf, about 11 inches long. Make 8 slices crosswise, *cutting to, but not through* bottom crust; make one cut lengthwise down center of loaf. Place on baking sheet.

Blend ½ cup butter or margarine, softened, with two 5-ounce jars sharp process cheese spread. Spread mixture between slices, over top, and sides. Sprinkle lightly with poppy seed *or* celery seed. Tie string around loaf to hold together. Bake at 400° about 15 minutes, or till cheese melts and bread is crusty. Serve hot like pan rolls with soup or salad. Makes 16.

Cheese Crescents

Prepare 2 cups packaged biscuit mix according to package directions. Knead 8 to 10 times. Roll out on floured surface to 14-inch circle.

Brush with 2 tablespoons butter, melted; sprinkle with 4 ounces sharp natural Cheddar cheese, shredded (1 cup). Cut in 10 wedges. Starting at wide end, roll each to form crescent. Put crescents, point down, on lightly greased baking sheet. Bake at 450° for 10 minutes or till brown. Serve hot. Makes 10.

Airy Cheese Rolls

    1 package active dry yeast
 1¾ cups milk, scalded
    4 ounces sharp process American
        cheese, shredded (1 cup)
  ¼ cup sugar
    2 tablespoons shortening
    4 cups sifted all-purpose flour
    1 beaten egg
  ½ cup cornmeal

Soften yeast in ¼ cup *warm* water. In large bowl of electric mixer combine hot milk, next 3 ingredients, and 1 teaspoon salt. Stir till cheese melts; cool to lukewarm. Add *2 cups* of the flour; beat 2 minutes at medium speed.

Add egg, yeast, cornmeal, and remaining flour. Beat 2 minutes. Cover; let rise in warm place till double, about 1¼ hours; stir down.

Fill greased 2½-inch muffin pans ½ full. Cover; let rise till double, about 45 minutes. Bake at 375° for 15 to 20 minutes. Makes 24.

Cheese-Topped Tomatoes

    5 large tomatoes
  ¼ cup soft bread crumbs
  ¼ cup shredded sharp process
        American cheese
    1 tablespoon butter, melted
        Snipped parsley

Slice off tops of tomatoes. Cut zigzag edges; season with salt and pepper. Combine crumbs, cheese, and butter; sprinkle over tomatoes. Garnish with parsley. Heat tomatoes on foil over *hot* coals (or bake at 375°) till warmed through. Serve immediately. Makes 5 servings.

Three-Cheese Mold

Mix 1½ teaspoons unflavored gelatin with ¼ cup cold water; heat till dissolved. Beat together 2 ounces blue cheese, crumbled (½ cup); 2 ounces natural Cheddar cheese, shredded (½ cup); and ½ cup cream-style cottage cheese.

Beat in ¼ cup dairy sour cream, 1½ teaspoons grated onion, ½ teaspoon Worcestershire sauce, and dissolved gelatin. Pour into 2-cup mold. Chill till firm. Serve with crackers.

Open the party with creamy Three-Cheese Mold, a do-ahead appetizer made with a trio of cheeses—blue, Cheddar, and cottage.

CHEESECAKE—A rich, creamy dessert prepared from unripened cheese combined with milk, eggs, and flavorings. Sometimes fruit juice or rind and/or nuts are added. Some are baked, others are chilled. Cheesecake has a velvety-smooth texture and is often served, topped with fresh fruit.

Making and serving cheesecake dates back to ancient times. Greeks and Romans featured it as a festival food. Essays were written on the merits of one kind of cheesecake over another. In the United States, cheesecake was so well liked by George Washington that Mrs. Washington included recipes in her cook book.

The cheese used in making this rich dessert varies from cream-style to dry-curd cottage, farmer's, pot or cream cheese. Today's cheesecakes are often made with a crumb crust on the bottom and part way up the sides. For this type of cake, a springform pan is best. When the sides of the pan are removed, the cheesecake stands ready for cutting.

Cheesecake may also be made in a pie plate—thus the name cheesecake pie. The crust may vary from a standard pastry to a crumb crust or puff pastry.

Speedy Cheesecake Pie

    1 cup graham cracker crumbs
    3 tablespoons butter, melted
    1 8-ounce package cream cheese,
        softened
    ½ cup sugar
    1 tablespoon lemon juice
    ½ teaspoon vanilla
    2 eggs
    1 cup dairy sour cream
    2 tablespoons sugar
    ½ teaspoon vanilla

Combine crumbs and butter. Press into buttered 8-inch pie plate, building up sides. Meanwhile, beat cream cheese till fluffy; blend in ½ cup sugar, lemon juice, ½ teaspoon vanilla, and dash salt. Add eggs, one at a time, beating well after each. Pour into crust. Bake at 325° for 30 minutes. Combine dairy sour cream, sugar, and vanilla; spoon over top of pie. Bake 10 minutes more. Cool. Chill several hours. Serve with fresh or frozen fruit, if desired.

Angel Cheesecake

A favorite when entertaining guests—

Crust:
    1 cup crushed zwieback
        (about 9 slices)
    2 tablespoons sugar
    2 tablespoons butter or margarine,
        melted
Filling:
    ½ cup sugar
    2 8-ounce packages cream cheese,
        softened
    1 teaspoon vanilla
    ¼ teaspoon salt
    ½ teaspoon grated lemon peel
    2 cups dairy sour cream
    5 egg yolks
    5 egg whites
    1 tablespoon lemon juice
    ½ cup sugar
Cherry Sauce:
    ½ cup sugar
    2 tablespoons cornstarch
        Dash salt
    1 20-ounce can frozen, pitted,
        tart red cherries (with syrup),
        thawed

Crust: Mix zwieback crumbs, 2 tablespoons sugar, and butter or margarine; press on bottom of *ungreased* 9-inch springform pan.

Filling: Gradually beat ½ cup sugar into softened cream cheese. Beat in vanilla, ¼ teaspoon salt, and grated lemon peel. Add sour cream and blend in egg yolks.

Beat egg whites with lemon juice to soft peaks; gradually add ½ cup sugar, beating till *very stiff*, but not dry, peaks form. Fold cheese mixture into egg whites. Pour into crumb-lined pan. Bake at 325° for 1¼ hours or till knife inserted off-center comes out clean.

Cool 10 minutes; run spatula around edge of top. (Cake settles slightly as it cools—loosening edge lets it do this evenly.) Cool thoroughly, about 1½ hours, before removing sides of pan. Chill thoroughly in refrigerator.

Pass *Cherry Sauce:* In saucepan combine ½ cup sugar, cornstarch, and dash salt. Stir in thawed cherries with syrup. Cook and stir over medium heat till mixture thickens and bubbles. Reduce heat; simmer 10 minutes. Chill before serving. Makes 10 servings.

Strawberry-Glazed Cheesecake

Crust:
- 1¾ cups fine graham-cracker crumbs (about 20 crackers)
- ¼ cup finely chopped walnuts
- ½ teaspoon ground cinnamon
- ½ cup butter or margarine, melted

Filling:
- 3 well-beaten eggs
- 2 8-ounce packages cream cheese, softened
- 1 cup sugar
- 2 teaspoons vanilla
- ½ teaspoon almond extract
- ¼ teaspoon salt
- 3 cups dairy sour cream

Glaze:
- 2 cups fresh strawberries
- ¾ cup water

. . .

- 2 tablespoons cornstarch
- ½ cup sugar
- Red food coloring

Crust: In bowl combine graham-cracker crumbs, walnuts, and cinnamon. Add melted butter or margarine; mix thoroughly. Press on bottom and sides of 9-inch springform pan. Sides should be about 1¾ inches high.

Filling: Combine eggs, cream cheese, ½ cup sugar, vanilla, almond extract, and salt; beat till smooth. Blend in sour cream. Pour into crumb crust. Bake at 375° about 35 minutes or just till set. Cool. Chill thoroughly, about 4 to 5 hours. (Filling will be soft.)

Glaze: Crush *1 cup* of the strawberries. Add water and cook 2 minutes; sieve. Mix cornstarch with ½ cup sugar; slowly stir in hot berry mixture. Bring to boiling, stirring constantly. Cook and stir till mixture is thick and clear. (Add a few drops red food coloring, if desired.) Cool to room temperature. Halve remaining strawberries. Place atop chilled cheesecake; pour strawberry glaze over. Chill about 2 hours. Makes 10 servings.

Cheesecake at its best

←Luscious Strawberry-Glazed Cheesecake—a winner at any table. In the summer, use fresh raspberries or blueberries for glaze.

For Cheesecake Supreme, pat dough on sides of springform pan. Rotate pan on edge to insure uniform thickness of crust.

Cheesecake Supreme

Crust:
- 1 cup sifted all-purpose flour
- ¼ cup sugar
- 1 teaspoon grated lemon peel

. . .

- ½ cup butter or margarine
- 1 slightly beaten egg yolk
- ¼ teaspoon vanilla

Filling:
- 5 8-ounce packages cream cheese, softened
- ¼ teaspoon vanilla
- ¾ teaspoon grated lemon peel
- 1¾ cups sugar
- 3 tablespoons all-purpose flour
- 4 or 5 eggs (1 cup)
- 2 egg yolks
- ¼ cup whipping cream

Crust: Mix first 3 ingredients. Cut in butter till crumbly. Add 1 beaten egg yolk and ¼ teaspoon vanilla; mix well. Pat ⅓ of the dough on bottom of 9-inch springform pan *with sides removed*. Bake at 400° for 8 minutes; cool. Butter sides of pan; attach to bottom. Pat remaining dough on sides 1¾ inches high.

Filling: Beat cheese; add ¼ teaspoon vanilla and ¾ teaspoon lemon peel. Mix 1¾ cups sugar, 3 tablespoons flour, and ¼ teaspoon salt; slowly add to cheese. Add eggs and 2 egg yolks, one at a time, beating well after each addition. Gently stir in whipping cream. Turn into pan. Bake at 450° for 12 minutes; reduce heat to 300°. Bake 55 minutes longer or till knife inserted off-center comes out clean. Cool 30 minutes; loosen sides of pan. Cool 30 minutes more; remove pan sides. Cool 2 hours; chill. Serves 12.

CHEESE STRAW—A long, narrow piece of pastry or dough flavored with cheese. The cheese may be incorporated into the dough or sprinkled on top of the dough. These tidbits are served as accompaniments to soups and salads or as appetizers.

Peanut-Cheese Straws

    ⅓ cup milk
    1 tablespoon sugar
    ½ teaspoon salt
    2 tablespoons butter or margarine
            • • •
    ¼ cup warm water
    1 package active dry yeast
    1 well-beaten egg
    1¾ to 2 cups sifted all-purpose
        flour
            • • •
    ¼ cup butter or margarine
    3 ounces sharp Cheddar cheese,
        shredded (¾ cup)
    ½ cup chopped dry roasted peanuts
    1 tablespoon water

Scald milk. Stir in sugar, salt, and 2 tablespoons butter; cool to lukewarm.

Measure warm water into mixing bowl. Sprinkle in yeast; stir till dissolved. Stir in lukewarm milk mixture. Setting aside 1 tablespoon of the beaten egg, stir in remaining egg and *half* the flour. Beat about 2 minutes at medium speed on electric mixer. Stir in enough additional flour to make a soft dough. Turn out onto lightly floured surface.

Knead till smooth and elastic, about 5 minutes. Place in greased bowl, turning to grease top of dough. Cover; let rise in warm place till double, about 30 minutes. Punch dough down and turn out onto floured surface. Roll out to a 10x6-inch rectangle, about ¼ inch thick. Dot center third with *2 tablespoons* of the remaining butter cut in small pieces, and sprinkle with *half* the shredded cheese. Fold one end of dough over to cover cheese. Dot with second 2 tablespoons butter and sprinkle with remaining cheese; fold last third of dough over to cover this cheese-butter layer.

Press edges of dough together firmly. Cover; let rest 20 minutes. Sprinkle board with *half* of the chopped nuts. Roll dough out over nuts into a 11x6-inch rectangle.

Combine reserved egg and 1 tablespoon water; brush over dough and sprinkle with remaining ¼ cup nuts. Cut dough in strips 6 inches long and ½ inch wide. Using spatula, place on greased baking sheet, about ½ inch apart. Let rise, uncovered, in a warm place, about 30 minutes. Bake at 400° till golden, about 10 to 12 minutes. Makes 2 dozen.

CHERIMOYA *(cher' uh moi' uh)*—A fancy, tropical fruit with a soft, custardlike center. It is heart-shaped, and the skin is green when the fruit is ripe. The seeds are not eaten. It is grown in Hawaii, California and Florida and is sometimes identified as a custard apple. (See also *Fruit.*)

CHERRIES JUBILEE—The name given to a glamorous dessert made using dark, sweet cherries flamed with brandy and spooned over ice cream. For a dramatic effect, dim the lights in the room just before lighting the brandy with a match.

Cherries Jubilee

Drain one 16-ounce can pitted dark sweet cherries (2 cups), reserving syrup. In saucepan blend ¼ cup sugar and 2 tablespoons cornstarch. Gradually stir in reserved cherry syrup, mixing well. Cook and stir over medium heat till mixture thickens and bubbles. Remove from heat and stir in cherries.

Turn cherry mixture into heat-proof bowl or top pan (blazer) of chafing dish. (Be sure bottom pan of chafing dish is filled with hot water; keep hot over flame.)

Heat ¼ cup brandy, kirsch, *or* cherry brandy in small metal pan with long handle. If desired, heated brandy can be poured into a large ladle. Carefully ignite heated brandy and pour over cherry mixture. Stir to blend brandy into sauce. Serve immediately over scoops of vanilla ice cream. Makes 2 cups sauce.

A dramatic ending to the meal

Cherries Jubilee, a gourmet dessert, makes → even the beginning cook in the kitchen turn into a cook-at-the-table showman.

CHERRY—A small, round or heart-shaped fruit having a single, smooth pit or stone belonging to the genus *Prunus*. The fruit is divided into two types—the sweet cherries and the sour or tart cherries, and both are related to the stone-fruit group that includes peaches, apricots, and plums.

It is surmised that cherry trees were first cultivated in China several thousand years ago; however, there is no proof of this. Records of cherries in Italy around 69 B.C. have been found.

Some authorities believe that the sweet cherry originated in the Caspian and Black Sea areas, and that birds may have carried the seeds of the sweet cherry tree from Asia, spreading the fruit over the European continent.

Cherries were brought to America by early settlers, and there are records of cherry trees having been here by 1629. Of course, the legend of George Washington and his cherry tree during the colonial period is familiar to all. Later, around the mid-1800's, the cherry industry got its start on the West Coast.

Nutritional value: Cherries are moderate in calorie yield. For the sour ones, about ½ cup raw cherries has 58 calories; ½ cup canned (water pack) has 43 calories; and ½ cup canned in syrup has 89 calories. For sweet cherries, 15 large ones have 70 calories, and ½ cup canned in syrup yields 89 calories. Cherries contain some vitamin A and some B vitamins.

Kinds of cherries: The most popular sweet cherries are the large, dark red Bing; the Lambert, a dark red cherry; the Tartarian, a small, purplish black cherry; and the Chapman, a large, round cherry. The favored light-colored sweet cherry is called the Napoleon or Royal Ann. This cherry has a light golden color with a red blush over it. It's used mainly for canning and is rarely found as a fresh fruit.

Of the sour cherries, the Montmorency is probably the most widely used variety in the United States. Other sour cherries include the English Morello and the Early Richmond. Most of the sour cherries are either canned or used cooked, while sweet cherries are usually eaten fresh.

Both types of cherries grow best where the temperatures are not extreme—neither too hot nor too cold. The spring blossoms are very susceptible to frost. Sour cherries, however, are a little more hardy than the sweet variety. Major areas of production for the sour cherries are in New York and the areas around the Great Lakes, mainly in Michigan and Wisconsin. Sweet cherry varieties come mainly from California, Oregon, and Washington.

The season for sweet cherries is from May to August, while the season for sour cherries is shorter, usually June and July.

How to select: Buy cherries that are fresh, firm, bright, and a good color for the particular variety. For most varieties of sweet cherries, a very dark color is a good indication of maturity. They should be glossy and have fresh stems. Cherries that are not ripe will be hard, will lack juiciness, and often have an acid taste. Overripe cherries will be soft, shriveled, dull in appearance, and may be leaking juice.

Cherries can be purchased year-round as canned and frozen products. Usually, the sour cherries will be pitted, while the sweet cherries can be purchased both pitted or unpitted. Ready-to-use cherry pie filling, candied cherries, cherry jams and preserves, and red or green maraschino cherries are grocery shelf staples.

How to store: After purchasing cherries, sort through them and discard any undesirable ones. Handle lightly as cherries are delicate and bruise easily. Refrigerate in plastic bags and use as soon as possible. Be sure to rinse them before using.

Cherries may be canned at home by either the cold-pack or hot-pack methods; they also freeze well. Sour cherries may be frozen in either a syrup or a sugar pack. To syrup-pack sour cherries, remove

Cherries used many luscious ways

Beginning at top of page is Cherry Meringue Cake, Cherry Bavarian, Creamy Cherry Pie, Cherry Dessert Salad, Molded Cherry Ring, and Cherry Shortcake Towers.

stems, wash, drain, and pit. Pack the cherries into freezer containers and cover the cherries with a cold, very heavy or extra heavy syrup, depending on the tartness of the fruit. Be sure to leave headspace; then seal, label, and freeze. To sugar-pack sour cherries, stem, wash, drain, and pit them. To each quart of fruit add ¾ cup sugar and mix lightly until the sugar is dissolved. Pack into freezer container—leave headspace. Seal, label, and freeze.

Sweet cherries can be syrup-packed. Stem, wash, drain, and pit them, if desired. Add ½ teaspoon ascorbic acid color keeper to each quart medium syrup. Pack the fruit into containers and cover it with syrup, leaving a headspace. Seal, label with contents and date, then freeze.

How to use: Sweet cherries are usually eaten fresh, but they also make delightful additions to fresh fruit salads and desserts. Cherries Jubilee is an excellent example of canned sweet cherries at their best. They are also delicious in sauces spooned over cake or in molded salads and desserts.

Cherry Bavarian

A two-layer beauty made in two separate molds—

> ¾ **cup sugar**
> 2 **envelopes unflavored gelatin**
>   **(2 tablespoons)**
> ¼ **teaspoon salt**
> 1½ **cups milk**
> 3 **beaten egg yolks**
> 1 **3-ounce package cream cheese, cut**
>   **up and softened**
> 1½ **cups light cream**
> ½ **teaspoon vanilla**
> ½ **teaspoon almond extract**
> 3 **stiffly beaten egg whites**
>   • • •
> 1 **16-ounce can pitted dark**
>   **sweet cherries**
> 1 **3-ounce package cherry-flavored**
>   **gelatin**
> ½ **cup whipping cream**

Creamy Layer: In saucepan combine sugar, unflavored gelatin, and salt. Stir in milk, then yolks. Cook and stir till thickened slightly.

With rotary beater, beat egg mixture into softened cream cheese until smooth. Add light cream, vanilla, and almond extract. Chill till gelatin mixture is partially set. Gently fold in stiffly beaten egg whites. Pour into 5-cup mold. Chill till firm, about 8 hours or overnight.

Cherry Layer: Drain cherries, reserving syrup. Cut up cherries. Add water to reserved syrup to make 1¾ cups. In saucepan combine syrup and cherry-flavored gelatin. Heat, stirring constantly, till gelatin dissolves. Chill till slightly thickened. Whip cream; fold into thickened cherry gelatin along with drained cherries. Pour into 3½-cup mold. Chill overnight. To serve, carefully unmold on top of Creamy Layer. Makes 8 to 10 servings.

Its attractive red color and ease of preparation makes canned cherry pie filling a good item to keep on the emergency shelf. In addition to using it in pies, it can be used in salads, desserts, or heated and served with cooked ham for the entrée.

Cherry Dessert Salad

In saucepan blend ⅓ cup sugar and 1 envelope unflavored gelatin (1 tablespoon). Stir in 1 cup unsweetened pineapple juice; heat and stir till gelatin is dissolved. Remove from heat. Beat into one 3-ounce package softened cream cheese till smooth. Add ¾ cup unsweetened pineapple juice and 1 tablespoon lemon juice. Chill till partially set. Whip till fluffy. Prepare one 2-ounce envelope dessert topping mix according to package directions. Fold into gelatin. Pour into 6½-cup mold. Chill till *almost* firm.

In small saucepan combine one 3-ounce package cherry-flavored gelatin and ¾ cup water. Heat till gelatin dissolves. Add one 21-ounce can cherry pie filling. Stir well. Chill till partially set, stirring occasionally. Spoon over cream cheese layer. Chill till the gelatin mixture is firm, about 6 hours or overnight.

Unmold and serve with *Custard Sauce:* In heavy saucepan mix 2 beaten eggs, dash salt, and ¼ cup sugar. Gradually stir in 2 cups milk, scalded and slightly cooled. Cook over low heat, stirring constantly, till mixture coats a metal spoon. Remove from heat. Cool pan at once in cold water; stir 1 or 2 minutes. Add 1 teaspoon vanilla. Chill. Makes 8 servings.

Cherry Meringue Cake

> 1 package 1-layer-size white cake
> mix
> ¾ teaspoon rum extract
> . . .
> 1 21-ounce can cherry pie filling
> 3 egg whites
> ½ teaspoon vanilla
> ¼ teaspoon cream of tartar
> 6 tablespoons sugar

Prepare cake following package directions adding rum flavoring to batter. Turn into a greased and floured 9x9x2-inch baking pan. Bake according to package directions. Cool.

Top with cherry pie filling. Beat egg whites with vanilla and cream of tartar till soft peaks form. Gradually add sugar, beating till stiff peaks form. Spread meringue over cherry filling, sealing to edges all around. Bake at 350° till peaks are golden brown, about 20 to 25 minutes. Trim with maraschino cherries, if desired. Makes 9 servings.

Cherry Parfaits

Layers of instant pudding, cherry pie filling, and almonds alternate in this luscious dessert—

> 1 cup milk
> 1 cup dairy sour cream
> ¼ teaspoon almond extract
> 1 3⅝- *or* 3¾-ounce package
> *instant* vanilla pudding mix
> . . .
> 1 21-ounce can cherry pie filling
> Toasted slivered almonds

In mixing bowl combine milk, sour cream, and almond extract. Add pudding mix and beat with rotary beater till creamy and well blended, about 2 minutes. Fill parfait glasses with alternate layers of pudding, cherry pie filling, and almonds; chill. Garnish with additional almonds. Makes 6 servings.

When sweetened, sour cherries are delicious in pies or shortcakes. They can be used in low-calorie salads. (See *Bing Cherry, Fruit, Maraschino Cherry, Montmorency Cherry* for additional information.)

Cherry Shortcake Towers

In mixing bowl sift together 2 cups sifted all-purpose flour, 1 tablespoon sugar, 4 teaspoons baking powder, and ½ teaspoon salt. Cut in ½ cup butter or margarine till mixture resembles coarse crumbs. Combine 1 beaten egg and ⅔ cup milk; add all at once to dry ingredients, stirring just to moisten.

Turn dough out onto floured surface. Knead gently about 30 seconds. Pat or roll dough to ½-inch thickness. Cut out 9 biscuits with floured 2½-inch cutter.

Bake on *ungreased* baking sheet at 450° for 8 to 10 minutes. Split shortcakes in half. Using three halves for each tower, fill and top with Cherry Topping. Garnish with whipped cream. Serve warm. Makes 6 servings.

Cherry Topping: In saucepan combine ⅓ cup sugar, 2 tablespoons cornstarch, and dash salt. Drain one 20-ounce can pitted tart red cherries (water pack), reserving juice. Add water to juice to make 1¼ cups liquid. Gradually stir cherry juice into sugar mixture; cook and stir till thickened and bubbly. Cook 1 minute more. Remove from heat. Add 1 tablespoon butter, drained cherries, 6 to 8 drops almond extract, 6 to 8 drops vanilla, and ¼ teaspoon red food coloring. Cool.

Molded Cherry Ring

A delicious, low calorie salad—

Drain one 20-ounce can pitted tart red cherries (water pack), reserving juice. Add enough water to juice to make 3 cups. In saucepan soften 2 envelopes unflavored gelatin (2 tablespoons) in juice mixture. Cook and stir over medium heat till gelatin is dissolved. Add non-caloric sweetener to equal ¾ cup sugar, 5 drops red food coloring, and drained cherries; bring the cherry mixture just to boiling.

Remove from heat; add ½ cup lemon juice. Chill till partially set, stirring occasionally. Fold in ¼ cup chopped celery, if desired. Turn into 5½-cup ring mold. Chill till firm.

Serve with *Fluffy Whipped Topping:* Pour ⅓ cup evaporated *skim* milk into mixing bowl. Chill the bowl and beaters. Add 1 tablespoon sugar and ¼ teaspoon vanilla. Whip with rotary beater or electric mixer to stiff peaks. *Use immediately.* Serves 8 or 9.

Who could resist a wedge of this tart, yet sweet Red Cherry Pie. The filling is an uncooked mixture of canned tart red cherries and can be ready by the time the pastry is rolled out.

2½ tBsp / ½ c. Juice

use tapioca recipe.

Red Cherry Pie

4 cups →

2 tBsp / c. Liquid

(3-4 TbSP)

1 ¼ ½ tsp.

- ¾ cup juice from cherries
- 3 cups canned pitted tart red cherries (water pack)
- 1 cup sugar   *¾ - 1 cup*
- 2 tablespoons quick-cooking tapioca
- 10 drops red food coloring
- 3 to 4 drops almond extract
  Pastry for 9-inch lattice top pie (See *Pastry*)
- 1 tablespoon butter or margarine

Combine juice from cherries, cherries, sugar, tapioca, food coloring, almond extract, and dash salt. Let stand 20 minutes.

Line 9-inch pie plate with pastry. Fill with cherry mixture. Dot with butter or margarine. Adjust lattice crust atop pie. Crimp edge high. Bake at 400° till crust is lightly browned, about 50 to 55 minutes.

Creamy Cherry Pie

Perfect for the February holidays—

Drain one 20-ounce can pitted tart red cherries (water pack), reserving ¾ cup juice. In saucepan mix together ⅔ cup sugar, ¼ cup cornstarch, and ¼ teaspoon salt. Gradually blend in reserved juice and ¼ cup water. Cook and stir till mixture thickens and bubbles. Remove from heat. Stir in ¼ teaspoon red food coloring, ¼ teaspoon almond extract, and drained cherries. Cool slightly.

Prepare one 9-inch pastry shell (See *Pastry*), crimping edges high. Bake. Reserving ¼ cup cherry mixture for garnish if desired, pour remaining cherries into the baked shell.

Prepare one 3⅝- or 3¾-ounce package *instant* vanilla pudding mix according to package directions *using only 1½ cups milk*. Let stand 1 to 2 minutes. Spoon over cherry filling. Chill. Garnish with reserved cherries.

Fresh Cherry Pie

Pastry for 8-inch lattice-top
pie (See *Pastry*)
3 cups pitted fresh ripe tart red
cherries
1 to 1½ cups sugar
¼ cup all-purpose flour
2 tablespoons butter or margarine

Line 8-inch pie plate with pastry. Combine cherries, sugar, flour, and dash salt. Turn into pastry-lined pie plate. Dot with butter or margarine. Adjust lattice top; seal. Bake at 400° for 50 to 55 minutes.

CHERRY TOMATO—A variety of tomato that is about the size and shape of a cherry and bright red in color. It usually ranges in size from 1 to 1½ inches but it may grow as large as 2 inches. It is sometimes available with its green calyx intact.

Cherry tomatoes add interesting color and shape contrasts to salads and vegetable platters. They make excellent hors d'oeuvres for eating as is or with a well-seasoned dip. (See also *Tomato*.)

CHERVIL *(chûr' vil)*—A delicate herb, related to the parsley family, with a light green, lacy, fernlike leaf. Chervil has a light, aromatic flavor, which some identify as faintly aniselike.

It is combined with more robust herbs in the familiar *bouquet garni* and is also an ingredient in *fines herbes*.

By itself, chervil is especially delicious in egg or cheese dishes and makes an attractive and pleasing garnish for buttered carrots. It is also a good addition to soups, salads, and stews.

In the United States chervil is grown commercially and can be found in many herb gardens. Chervil can also be purchased as dried leaves. (See also *Herb*.)

CHESS PIE—The name given to a rich, buttery, sugary, custard-type pie containing a bit of lemon juice added for flavor. The filling sometimes includes raisins and nuts and is baked in a rich pastry shell. This delightful dessert is an old-fashioned Southern favorite. (See also *Pie*.)

Chess Pie

Small pieces of this pie are usually served—

Cream ½ cup butter and 2 cups sugar. Beat in 1 tablespoon all-purpose flour and 1 tablespoon yellow cornmeal. Add 5 well-beaten eggs, 1 cup milk, 2 tablespoons lemon juice, and 1 teaspoon vanilla; beat. Pour into 1 unbaked Rich Pastry Shell. Bake at 350° till knife inserted in center of pie comes out clean, about 55 minutes.

Rich Pastry Shell: Sift together 1 cup sifted all-purpose flour, ¼ teaspoon salt, and ¼ teaspoon baking powder. Cut in 6 tablespoons butter till size of small peas.

Gradually add 3 to 4 tablespoons milk, mixing till dough can be formed into a ball. Roll out and fit into 9-inch pie plate (have pastry edges crimped high because filling is generous).

CHESTNUT—A sweet nut that grows in a prickly burr. Since a blight destroyed many chestnut trees in America several decades ago, most chestnuts found in the markets are imported from Italy.

Chestnuts are cooked before eating, usually by roasting or boiling. They can be eaten plain or used in other mixtures.

To roast fresh chestnuts: with a sharp knife, make cross-slits on the flat side of each chestnut. Place in a shallow baking pan and roast at 400° for 15 minutes, tossing occasionally. Serve piping hot.

To boil fresh chestnuts: with a sharp knife, slash the flat side of each chestnut. Place in a saucepan of cold water. Bring to boiling; boil 8 to 10 minutes. Remove from heat. With slotted spoon remove 3 or 4 chestnuts at a time from water. Peel off the outer shells and the brown inner skins, taking care to keep the chestnuts whole. For ease in peeling, leave unpeeled chestnuts in warm cooking water till peeled.

Chestnuts can also be purchased in cans, either whole or puréed. Puréed or chopped, cooked chestnuts make a delicious addition to poultry stuffing. Preserved chestnuts are also available, either whole nuts or in pieces. Preserved marrons, called *marrons glacés,* are large, special chestnuts candied in France. These are delicious confections. (See also *Nut*.)

CHICKEN

*Ideas for using this international favorite
ranging from simple soups to exotic entrées.*

The sweet, delicately flavored flesh of this domesticated fowl is a most versatile food. Chicken is tasty enough to be enjoyed eaten alone, yet delicate enough to blend well with so many other foods that it can be eaten often without becoming boring. Because of its flavor and digestibility, chicken is a favorite with all ages.

Today's chickens descended from fowl that were cackling in the jungles of southwestern Asia thousands of years ago. The first time our ancestors had the ingenious idea of using them for food was about 1400 B.C. Since then, man has domesticated the bird and chicken raising has spread extensively. Spanish explorers brought them to the Americas in the 1550's and the English brought chickens to their American colonies in the 1600's.

Despite this long use of chickens, it was not until the nineteenth century that breeders began to improve the bird. Through developments in breeding and feeding, a meatier, more flavorful chicken can be produced in only 65 days. Chickens no longer need be Sunday treats—now they can be everyday fare.

Nutritional value: Chicken is an excellent source of good quality protein, yet is low in calories. Minerals, such as calcium, phosphorus, and iron, plus the B vitamins are found in this meat. Light meat has less fat, iron, and the B vitamins, riboflavin and thiamine, than the dark meat, but more of the B vitamin, niacin. Young broiler-fryers will have even less fat than the older roasting and stewing chickens.

One serving of broiler-fryer before cooking averages 150 calories and of a roasting chicken averages 300 calories. Fat is found in layers just under the skin rather than distributed through the flesh. Calories can be minimized by removing the skin and using a recipe that does not add extra fat.

Kinds of chickens: Basically, chickens are divided into five categories according to age and weight. These categories are:

Broiler-fryer or fryer—Young tender birds weighing 1½ to 3½ pounds. Broiler-fryers may be roasted, simmered, baked, fried, grilled, or broiled.

Capon—Castrated roosters weighing 4 to 7 pounds and having large amounts of tender, flavorful white meat. They are roasted.

Roaster—Tender birds that weigh 3 to 5 pounds. They are roasted.

Stewing chicken—Mature, less tender birds weighing 2½ to 5 pounds and having more fat. Cook in liquid.

Cornish game hen—The smallest and youngest type of chicken, weighing 1½ pounds or less. Roast, broil, or fry these. Stuff before roasting, if desired.

Chickens are readily available fresh, frozen, and canned. Practically all that are sold in supermarkets are ready to cook. This means they are cleaned, eviscerated, and free from pinfeathers.

Fresh and frozen chickens are packaged as whole birds or as several pieces of one part, such as breasts or wings. Frozen products also include precooked chicken, either in pieces, as entrées with a complete dinner, or as the entrée alone; for instance, chicken with dumplings.

Childhood favorite turns appetizer

← Dunking Dipper's Drumsticks, either hot or cold, into Zippy Pineapple, Royal Red, and Creamy Dill Sauces will be a hit at parties.

Canned products cover a wide range of items. Whole or boned pieces of chicken are available in cans. Foods made with chicken, including entrées, gravy, baby food, soup, and sandwich spread, are canned to serve many purposes. And new products are constantly being developed.

How to select: Evaluate the cost in time and money when deciding which type of chicken to buy. Canned and frozen prepared dishes cost more than those made at home, but may be worth the expense if you have little time for cooking or want to be prepared for emergency meals. Packages of pieces are more expensive than whole chickens; again, the cost may be justified because like pieces cook in the same amount of time, or because your family prefers wings, legs, or breasts.

When buying fresh chicken, choose those with white or yellow skin that is thin, moist, and tender. Feel the flesh to see that it's plump and firm. Examine the breastbone to see if it is soft and flexible. Avoid chickens with off-odors for they are probably not fresh.

Grade and inspection marks are found on the label, wrapper, wing tag, or package insert and indicate the quality of the chicken. The United States Department of Agriculture grades A, B, and C appear in a shield-shaped mark. These grades indicate quality; Grade A is the finest and the most widely sold. A circular mark reading "Inspected for Wholesomeness by USDA" assures the consumer of a healthy bird processed under sanitary conditions. Federal inspection is required on all poultry transported across state lines.

Roast Chicken Elegante turns an ordinary meal into a banquet. Gingery orange sauce glazes the outside while a superbly seasoned stuffing of wild and long-grain rice bakes inside the bird.

How much chicken to buy for a serving

Broiler-fryer................¼ to ½ bird
Capon, roaster, stewing.....½ pound
Cornish game hen..........1 bird
Breast halves..............⅓ pound
Whole legs................⅓ to ½ pound
Drumsticks or thighs........⅓ to ½ pound
Wings....................¾ pound
Backs....................⅔ pound

How to store: Refrigerate fresh chicken as soon as possible. Remove package of giblets from cavity of whole birds, cover the bird loosely in waxed paper or clear plastic wrap, and place in the coldest section of the refrigerator for one or two days. If not used within this time, freeze in moisture-vaporproof wrapping either whole or cut into parts. Frozen uncooked chicken will keep in the freezer 12 months.

Leftover cooked chicken should be chilled immediately and used in one or two days. It can be frozen for two to four months. Fried chicken, however, does not freeze satisfactorily. Never chill or freeze chicken with stuffing in it.

How to prepare: Chicken requires some basic preparation before cooking. Cut into desired pieces and rinse in cold water. Drain and if it is to be cooked in fat, dry to prevent spattering.

Frozen chicken is usually thawed before cooking. However, it can be roasted, fried, braised, or stewed without thawing, but this requires extra cooking time.

The best way to thaw chicken is in its original wrap, on a tray or pan in the refrigerator. A whole, three-pound bird will take about 12 hours to thaw. If you're in a hurry, thaw chicken in cold water: leave the chicken wrapped and immerse in cold water. Change the water often. It will take ½ to 1 hour to thaw small birds. Another method is to let the wrapped chicken stand at room temperature but do not try this in warm weather—it might spoil. Allow two or three hours per pound.

How to use: Chicken's wide acceptance makes it an excellent choice to serve at any meal. It's a welcome favorite to all ages in the family at a hearty breakfast, at dinner, or during a raid on the refrigerator. When serving guests whose food preferences are not known to you, chicken is one of your safest choices for the entrée.

Chicken roasting chart

Chicken	Ready-To-Cook Weight	Oven Temp.	Roasting Time Stuffed and Unstuffed	Special Instructions
Broiler-fryer Roaster	1½-2 pounds 2-2½ pounds 2½-3 pounds 3-4 pounds 4-5 pounds	375° 375° 375° 375° 375°	¾-1 hr. 1-1¼ hrs. 1¼-1½ hrs. 1½-2 hrs. 2-2½ hrs.	Stuff, if desired, and truss. Place bird breast up on rack in shallow roasting pan. Rub skin thoroughly with salad oil. Roast uncovered. Brush dry areas of skin occasionally with pan drippings.
Capon	4-7 pounds	375°	2-3 hrs.	Same as above.
Cornish Game Hen	1-1½ pounds	375°	1½ hrs.	Prepare as above. Roast, loosely covered, for ½ hour, then, roast uncovered till done, about 1 hour. If desired, occasionally baste with melted butter or glaze the last hour.

Whole chicken

Whole chickens are ideal for roasting. This method takes little preparation time and produces a juicy, tender bird. For holiday meals, chicken is a good substitute for the traditional turkey—especially if your guest list is not large, or if some would prefer an entrée other than turkey.

Stuffed whole chickens make a grand meal whether served during the holidays, when entertaining, or for a family meal. Remember: the bird is not stuffed until just before it is roasted, and any leftover stuffing is put into the refrigerator as soon as possible after the meal.

Cornish Hens with Rice Stuffing

       2   1- to 1½-pound ready-to-cook
           Cornish game hens
       ⅔   cup uncooked packaged precooked
           rice
       2   tablespoons dried currants
       2   tablespoons claret
       ½   teaspoon sugar
       ¼   teaspoon salt
           Dash pepper
           Dash ground nutmeg
           Dash ground allspice
       2   tablespoons slivered almonds,
           toasted
           Salad oil
           Wine Glaze

Season game hens inside and out with salt and pepper. In saucepan combine rice and ½ cup water; mix to moisten. Bring quickly to a boil, fluffing rice with a fork once or twice. Add currants, wine, sugar, ¼ teaspoon salt, dash pepper, nutmeg, and allspice. Cover and return to boiling, remove from heat. Let stand 10 minutes. Add slivered almonds.

Lightly stuff birds with rice mixture. Place breast up on rack in shallow baking pan. Brush with salad oil. Roast, covered, at 375° for 30 minutes. Uncover and continue roasting till drumstick can be easily twisted in socket, about 1 hour; occasionally basting with wine glaze. Makes 2 servings.

Wine Glaze: Combine ¼ cup claret; 3 tablespoons butter or margarine, melted; and 1½ teaspoons lemon juice. Brush hens with glaze.

Roast Chicken Elegante

Festive for holiday or guest meal—

       1   3-ounce can broiled sliced
           mushrooms
       1   6-ounce package long-grain and
           wild rice mix
       1   tablespoon instant minced onion
       1   14-ounce can chicken broth
       2   3-pound ready-to-cook whole
           broiler-fryer chickens
                · · ·
       ½   cup light corn syrup
       2   tablespoons thinly slivered
           orange peel
       ¼   cup orange juice
       ¼   teaspoon ground ginger
                · · ·
       1   orange, cut in thick slices
           Butter or margarine
           Cranberry-orange relish

Drain mushrooms, reserving liquid. In medium saucepan combine rice mix and onion; stir in chicken broth and the reserved mushroom liquid. Cook according to package directions. Stir in mushrooms. Lightly stuff chickens with rice mixture; skewer shut.

Tie drumsticks to tail. Place birds, breast side up, on rack in shallow baking pan; tuck wings under or tie across back. Roast stuffed chickens at 375° for 1½ hours.

Meanwhile, combine corn syrup, orange peel, orange juice, and ground ginger. Brush chickens with corn syrup glaze and roast 15 minutes longer. Remove cord and skewers from each chicken; let chickens stand on warm serving platter a few minutes before carving.

For garnish, cook thick orange slices in butter till warm; then top with cranberry-orange relish. Arrange slices and parsley, if desired, around chickens. Serves 8 to 10.

Sections of chicken

Chicken cut into halves, quarters, or pieces can be prepared in countless ways. Halves and quarters are a convenient size to broil or barbecue. Cut into smaller pieces, chicken combines well with other ingredients or makes a handy size to fry, stew, or bake. These pieces are also ideal for serving.

They are easy to handle, even for children, and one or two meaty pieces are a good amount for most servings.

Gourmet dishes around the world are made using cut-up chicken. The *arroz con pollo* of Spain and Mexico, *Kiev* of Russia, *coq au vin* of France, and *cacciatore* of Italy are but a few examples.

Basic Broiled Chicken

Select two ready-to-cook broiler-fryer chickens (not over 2½ pounds each); split each chicken in half lengthwise or quarter. Brush with salad oil or melted shortening. Season to taste with salt and pepper.

Place, skin side down, in broiled pan (no rack). Broil 5 to 7 inches from heat, about 20 minutes or till lightly browned. Brush occasionally with salad oil. Turn; broil 20 minutes longer. When drumstick moves easily, chicken is done. Makes 4 servings.

Honey Barbecued Broilers

Display gourmet skills at an outdoor barbecue or use same sauce when broiling chicken indoors—

    ¾ cup butter or margarine
    ⅓ cup vinegar
    ¼ cup honey
    2 cloves garlic, minced
    2 teaspoons salt
    ½ teaspoon dry mustard
    ½ teaspoon dried marjoram leaves,
        crushed
      Dash freshly ground pepper
        • • •
    3 2-pound ready-to-cook broiler-
        fryer chickens, halved lengthwise

Combine butter or margarine, vinegar, honey, garlic, salt, mustard, marjoram, and pepper; mix well. Place chicken, skin side down, on grill. Tuck wings under. Broil over low coals for 20 minutes.* Turn halves over; generously brush broiled side of chicken with honey sauce. Broil 10 minutes, turn, and brush second side with sauce. Broil 5 minutes more. Remove from heat. Just before serving, brush again with honey sauce. Makes 6 servings.

Or, use method for Basic Broiled Chicken.

Delicious Baked Chicken

    1 2½- to 3-pound ready-to-cook
        broiler-fryer chicken, cut up
    2 tablespoons shortening
        • • •
    ½ cup sliced onion
    1 clove garlic, minced
    1 16-ounce can tomatoes
        • • •
    ¼ cup grated Parmesan cheese
    3 tablespoons all-purpose flour
    ½ cup dairy sour cream

Salt and pepper chicken; brown in hot shortening. Place in 12x7½x2-inch baking dish. Cook onion and garlic in 1 tablespoon drippings till tender. Add tomatoes; bring to boiling. Pour over chicken; cover and bake at 350° for 1 hour. Remove chicken to platter; sprinkle with cheese. In saucepan blend flour into sour cream; stir in drippings. Cook and stir till mixture thickens. Serve over chicken. Serves 4.

Oven Herb Chicken

Cut up one 2½- to 3-pound ready-to-cook broiler-fryer chicken. Combine 1 envelope onion salad dressing mix; ½ cup butter or margarine, softened; and 1 teaspoon paprika. With spatula spread mixture over chicken pieces, then roll in ¾ cup fine dry bread crumbs. Sprinkle with paprika. Bake, skin side up, in greased large shallow baking pan at 375° till done, about 1 hour. Do not turn pieces during baking. Makes 4 servings.

Barbecued Chicken

In skillet brown slowly in ¼ cup salad oil, one 2½- to 3-pound ready-to-cook broiler-fryer chicken, cut up. Place in 12x7½x2-inch baking dish. To skillet add ½ cup chopped onion and ¼ cup chopped celery; cook till tender. Add ½ cup catsup, ⅓ cup water, 2 tablespoons lemon juice, 1 tablespoon *each* brown sugar, Worcestershire sauce, vinegar, and prepared mustard. Season with salt and pepper. Simmer 15 minutes; skim off excess fat. Pour sauce over chicken. Bake, uncovered, at 325° till done, about 1¼ hours. Baste 3 or 4 times during baking. Makes 3 or 4 servings.

Perfect Fried Chicken

    1/3 cup all-purpose flour
    1 teaspoon paprika
    1 teaspoon salt
    1/4 teaspoon pepper
    1 2½- to 3-pound ready-to-cook
        broiler-fryer chicken, cut up
    Shortening for frying

Combine flour, paprika, salt, and pepper in paper or plastic bag; add 2 or 3 pieces of chicken at a time and shake. Heat shortening (1/4 inch deep in skillet) till a drop of water sizzles.

Brown meaty pieces first; then add remaining pieces (don't crowd). Brown one side; turn with tongs. When lightly browned, 15 to 20 minutes, reduce heat; cover tightly. (If cover isn't tight, add 1 tablespoon water.) Cook until tender, 30 to 40 minutes. Cook, uncovered, during the last 10 minutes. Makes 4 servings.

Note: Add ½ cup fine dry bread crumbs to flour for more crusty coating.

Oven Fried Chicken

Cut up one 2½- to 3-pound ready-to-cook broiler-fryer chicken. Dip pieces in ½ cup melted butter or margarine; roll in mixture of 2 cups crushed potato chips (*or* 2 cups crushed barbecue chips, or crushed cornflakes, or 3 cups crisp rice cereal, crushed), 1/4 teaspoon garlic salt, and dash pepper. Place pieces, skin side up, not touching, in greased large shallow baking pan. Sprinkle with remaining butter and crumbs. Bake at 375° till done, about 1 hour. Do not turn. Makes 4 servings.

Dipper's Drumsticks

    3/4 cup all-purpose flour
    1 tablespoon paprika
    18 to 24 chicken drumsticks
            •   •   •
    Shortening for frying
    Zippy Pineapple Sauce
    Royal Red Sauce
    Creamy Dill Sauce

Combine flour, 1 tablespoon salt, paprika, and 1/4 teaspoon pepper in plastic or paper bag; add 2 or 3 drumsticks at a time, and shake to coat.

Heat shortening (1/4 inch deep in skillet) till a drop of water sizzles. Brown drumsticks on all sides, avoiding overcrowding—use 2 skillets, if necessary. Turn chicken with tongs. When lightly browned, 15 to 20 minutes, reduce heat; cover tightly. (If cover is not tight, add 1 tablespoon water.) Cook 30 minutes; uncover and cook 10 minutes longer. Serve drumsticks hot or chilled with sauces.

Zippy Pineapple Sauce: In saucepan combine one 12-ounce jar (1 cup) pineapple preserves, 1/4 cup prepared mustard, and 1/4 cup prepared horseradish; blend together. Heat the sauce through. Makes 1½ cups sauce.

Royal Red Sauce: In saucepan combine ½ cup extra-hot catsup and 6 tablespoons butter or margarine; heat just till blended. Makes about 3/4 cup Royal Red Sauce.

Creamy Dill Sauce: Combine ½ cup dairy sour cream, 1/4 cup mayonnaise or salad dressing, and 1/4 teaspoon dried dillweed, crushed. Let sauce stand at room temperature for 1 hour before serving to blend flavors. Makes 3/4 cup.

Chicken Parisienne

    6 medium chicken breasts
    ½ cup dry white wine
    1 10½-ounce can condensed
        cream of mushroom soup
    1 3-ounce can sliced mushrooms,
        drained
    Paprika
    1 cup dairy sour cream
    Hot cooked rice

Place chicken breasts, skin side up, in 12x7½x2-inch baking dish; sprinkle with salt. Blend wine into mushroom soup; add mushrooms and pour over chicken. Bake at 350° for 1 to 1¼ hours. Remove chicken to heated platter; sprinkle with paprika. Pour sauce into saucepan; blend in sour cream and heat gently till hot. Serve mushroom sauce over chicken and hot cooked rice. Makes 6 servings.

Grilled to perfection

Brush chicken halves with honey sauce that →
has a hint of herbs to accentuate the delicate flavor of Honey Barbecued Broilers.

Rolled Chicken Washington

½ cup finely chopped fresh
    mushrooms
2 tablespoons butter or margarine
2 tablespoons all-purpose flour
½ cup light cream
    Dash cayenne
5 ounces sharp natural Cheddar
    cheese, shredded (1¼ cups)
6 boned whole chicken breasts
    All-purpose flour
2 slightly beaten eggs
¾ cup fine dry bread crumbs

Cook mushrooms in butter 5 minutes. Blend in the 2 tablespoons flour; stir in cream. Add ¼ teaspoon salt and cayenne; cook and stir till mixture is very thick. Stir in cheese; cook over very low heat, stirring till cheese melts. Turn into pie plate. Cover; chill 1 hour. Cut into 6 pieces; shape into short sticks.

Remove skin from chicken breasts. Place each piece, boned side up, between clean plastic wrap. (Overlap meat where split.) Pound out from the center with wood mallet to form cutlets not quite ¼ inch thick. Peel off wrap. Sprinkle meat with salt. Place a cheese stick on each piece. Tucking in the sides, roll as for jelly roll. Press to seal well. Dust rolls with flour; dip in egg, then in crumbs. Cover and chill thoroughly—at least 1 hour.

An hour before serving, fry rolls in deep, hot fat (375°) for 5 minutes; drain on paper toweling. Bake in shallow baking dish at 325° for 30 to 45 minutes. Serves 6.

Rolled Chicken Breasts

3 large chicken breasts, boned,
    skinned, and halved lengthwise
6 thin slices boiled ham
6 ounces natural Swiss cheese,
    cut in 6 sticks
¼ cup all-purpose flour
2 tablespoons butter or margarine
1 teaspoon chicken flavored gravy
    base
1 3-ounce can sliced mushrooms,
    drained
⅓ cup sauterne
2 tablespoons all-purpose flour
    Toasted sliced almonds

Place chicken pieces, boned side up, on cutting board. Working from center out, pound chicken lightly with wooden mallet to make cutlets about ¼ inch thick. Sprinkle with salt. Place a ham slice and a cheese stick on each cutlet. Tuck in sides of each and roll up as for jelly roll, pressing to seal well. Skewer or tie securely. Coat rolls with the ¼ cup flour; brown in the butter. Remove chicken rolls to a 11x7x1½-inch baking pan.

In small skillet combine ½ cup water, the gravy base, mushrooms, and wine. Heat, stirring in any crusty bits from skillet. Pour mixture over chicken in baking pan. Cover and bake at 350° till tender, about 1 to 1¼ hours. Transfer chicken to serving platter. Blend the 2 tablespoons flour with ½ cup cold water. Add to gravy in baking pan. Cook and stir till thickened. Pour a little gravy over chicken; garnish with toasted sliced almonds. Pass remaining gravy. Makes 6 servings.

Chicken with Dumplings

Prepare Stewed Chicken (*see page 486*). When chicken is almost tender, sift together 1 cup sifted all-purpose flour, 2 teaspoons baking powder, and ½ teaspoon salt. Combine ½ cup milk and 2 tablespoons salad oil; add to dry ingredients. Stir just to moisten. Drop from tablespoon directly onto chicken in boiling stock. (Do not let batter drop in liquid.)

Cover tightly; return to boiling. Reduce heat (don't lift cover); simmer till done, about 12 to 15 minutes. Remove dumplings and chicken to hot platter. Keep hot while preparing Chicken Gravy. Makes 10 dumplings.

Chicken Gravy: Strain broth from chicken. Measure 1 quart into medium saucepan. Heat to boiling. Combine ½ cup all-purpose flour and 1 cup cold water; gradually add to broth, mixing well. Cook, stirring constantly, till mixture is thickened and bubbly. Season with 1½ teaspoons salt and ⅛ teaspoon pepper. Pour over chicken and dumplings. Makes 6 to 8 servings.

Surprise waits inside crisp chicken

Cutting into Rolled Chicken Washington reveals the hot cheese. Garnish this entrée with grapes and parsley. Serve with baked rice.

Ground or cubed chicken

Tasty sandwich spreads, salads, casseroles, appetizers, and soups are made with ground or cubed chicken. The meat can be purchased in cans or prepared by cubing a stewed chicken. Converting leftover chicken into a new dish by grinding or cubing will enable you to vary your menus and keep them interesting and creative. If preferred, freeze the ground or cubed leftovers for later use. (See also *Poultry*.)

Stewed Chicken

Excellent to use in salads or casseroles—

    1 5- to 6-pound ready-to-cook
        stewing chicken, cut up, *or*
        2 large broiler-fryer
        chickens, cut up
    2 sprigs parsley
    4 celery branches with leaves,
        cut up
    1 carrot, peeled and sliced
    1 small onion, cut up
    2 teaspoons salt
    ¼ teaspoon pepper

Place chicken pieces in Dutch oven or large kettle with enough water to cover (about 2 quarts). Add remaining ingredients. Cover; bring to boiling and cook over low heat about 2½ hours, or till tender. Leave chicken on bones in liquid for Chicken with Dumplings. Or, remove meat from bones. This will yield about 5 cups diced chicken for salads or casseroles.

Chinese Chicken

    1 medium green pepper, cut in
        strips
    1 cup bias cut celery
    2 tablespoons butter or margarine
    1 10½-ounce can condensed cream
        of chicken soup
    ⅓ cup water
    2 tablespoons soy sauce
    2 cups cubed cooked chicken
    1 16-ounce can chop suey
        vegetables, drained
      Hot cooked rice

In a saucepan cook green pepper and celery in butter till crisp-tender. Stir in cream of chicken soup, water, and soy sauce. Add chicken and chop suey vegetables; heat through. Serve over hot cooked rice. Pass additional soy sauce, if desired. Makes 6 servings.

Club Chicken Casserole

    ¼ cup butter or margarine
    ¼ cup all-purpose flour
    1 14½-ounce can evaporated milk
    1 cup chicken broth
    ½ cup water
    3 cups cooked long grain rice
    2½ cups diced cooked chicken
    1 3-ounce can sliced mushrooms,
        drained
    ⅓ cup chopped green pepper
    ¼ cup chopped canned pimiento
    1½ teaspoons salt
    ¼ cup toasted slivered almonds
        (optional)

In saucepan melt butter; blend in flour. Add evaporated milk, chicken broth, and water; cook quickly, stirring constantly, till thickened and bubbly. Add rice, chicken, mushrooms, green pepper, pimiento, and salt. Pour mixture into a greased 2-quart casserole. Bake, uncovered, at 350° for 40 minutes. If desired, top with almonds. Serves 8 to 10.

Chicken Chip Bake

    2 cups cubed cooked chicken
    2 cups sliced celery
    ¾ cup mayonnaise or salad dressing
    ⅓ cup toasted slivered almonds
    2 teaspoons grated onion
    2 tablespoons lemon juice
    ½ teaspoon salt
        •   •   •
    2 ounces process American cheese,
        shredded (½ cup)
    1 cup crushed potato chips

Combine all ingredients except shredded cheese and potato chips. Pile lightly in 1½-quart casserole. Sprinkle with cheese, then with potato chips. Bake at 425° till heated through, about 20 minutes. Makes 5 or 6 servings.

Chicken-Noodle Soup

In saucepan bring 3 cups chicken broth to a boil. (Use broth from Stewed Chicken, canned chicken broth, or chicken bouillon cubes dissolved in water.) Add 1 cup noodles and cook till noodles are tender. Makes 4 servings.

CHICKEN-FLAVORED BASE—A blend of chicken extract and flavoring used to make soup, gravy, and broth or to season meat and vegetable mixtures. The base is available as a liquid, as instant granules, as a paste, and in gravy mixes. (See also *Gravy.*)

CHICKEN-FRIED—A method of cooking in which the food is coated with seasoned flour or dipped in egg, then crumbs and pan-fried. This coating produces a brown crust over the food. Thin pieces of meat, such as round steak, are prepared in this manner. These must be pounded to tenderize if not tender. Creamy gravy is usually served with chicken-fried meat.

Chicken-Fried Steak

  1½ pounds beef top round steak,
         ½ inch thick
    1 beaten egg
    1 tablespoon milk
    1 cup fine cracker crumbs
    ¼ cup salad oil

Pound steak ¼ inch thick; cut into 6 serving pieces. Blend egg and milk. Dip meat in egg mixture, then in crumbs. Slowly brown meat in hot oil, turning once. Cover; cook over low heat till tender, about 45 to 60 minutes. Season with salt and pepper. Makes 6 servings.

CHICKEN LIVER—A small, delicately flavored liver used in the same way as other animal livers. They can be fried, broiled, used in casseroles and meat dishes, or added to giblet gravy and stuffing. Cook till just done, for overcooking toughens the meat and dries out the flavor.

Chicken livers contain B vitamins, iron, and large amounts of vitamin A. Yet, one medium liver has only 75 calories.

Chicken-Fried Steak combines a crisp crust with juicy, tender meat. Serve as a main dish with a favorite vegetable, boiled and sliced. Add a tangy, molded salad, hot bread, and dessert of parfaits with cookies.

Entice guests or family with Chicken Livers Portugal. The combination of chicken livers topped with a wine-flavored sauce and wild rice adds a gourmet touch to the meal.

Packages of the livers can be purchased fresh or frozen. When preparing whole chickens, the livers may be set aside, if desired, and frozen until there are enough collected to use them as a main dish.

Chicken Livers Portugal

> 5 **tablespoons butter or margarine**
> 1 **clove garlic, minced**
> 2 **tablespoons minced onion**
> 2 **tablespoons all-purpose flour**
> 1 **cup canned condensed beef broth**
> 1 **pound chicken livers**
> 3 **tablespoons Madeira or Marsala**

Melt *3 tablespoons* butter in a heavy saucepan or skillet; add garlic and onion. Cook till onion is tender but not brown. Blend in *2 tablespoons* flour. Add beef broth; cook and stir till sauce is smooth and thickened. Combine the remaining flour, ½ teaspoon salt, and dash pepper; coat livers with flour mixture.

In medium skillet brown livers quickly in the remaining butter; gently stir livers and wine into the sauce. Heat through and serve livers over wild rice, if desired. Serves 4.

Chicken Livers en Brochette

> ¾ **pound fresh *or* frozen chicken livers, thawed (about 15)**
> 3 **tablespoons butter or margarine, melted**
> ⅔ **cup fine dry bread crumbs**
> 2 **teaspoons butter or margarine**
> ½ **teaspoon onion powder**
>   **Dash cayenne**
> 2 **tablespoons Dijon-style mustard**
> 1 **tablespoon catsup**
> 2 **teaspoons Worcestershire sauce**

Dip chicken livers in the 3 tablespoons melted butter or margarine; coat with the bread crumbs. Thread on 3 skewers. Place on greased broiler rack; broil 6 inches from heat for about 3 minutes on each side or till livers are tender.

Meanwhile, in small saucepan melt 2 teaspoons butter; stir in onion powder, cayenne, mustard, catsup, and Worcestershire sauce. Heat just to boiling. Serve with livers. Makes 3 main dish servings.

Chicken Livers and Rice

> 1⅓ **cups packaged precooked rice**
> ½ **pound chicken livers, cut up**
>   **Butter or margarine**
> 1 **10-ounce package frozen chopped spinach, thawed**
> 2 **tablespoons butter or margarine**
> 2 **tablespoons Burgundy**
> 4 **ounces sharp natural Cheddar cheese, shredded (1 cup)**

Cook rice according to package directions. Brown livers in a small amount of butter. Combine rice, livers, spinach, the 2 tablespoons butter, wine, ½ teaspoon salt, dash pepper, and cheese. Spoon into a 1½-quart casserole. Bake, covered, at 350° for 25 minutes. Garnish with additional shredded Cheddar cheese, if desired. Makes 5 or 6 servings.

CHICK-PEA—A pealike seed, also known as garbanzo. (See also *Garbanzo*.)

CHICORY (*chik' uh rē*)—A thick-rooted herb with bright blue flowers. The plant is cultivated for its roots and bitter leaves.

Chicory is known by several names. Its old name was succory. Witloof, endive, Belgian endive, French endive, and escarole are sometimes confused with chicory and mistakenly purchased as such. The characteristics which distinguish chicory

Skewer chicken livers and broil for a crunchy main dish or appetizer. Serve Chicken Livers en Brochette with the savory sauce.

from the flat or bushy endive and escarole are its thin, elongated stalk, tightly folded leaves, and color—which is usually bleached white during growth.

Nutritional value: Chicory contains some vitamin A and minerals. The calories are low—only four in ten small leaves.

How to use: Chicory leaves that are crisp, bright, and fresh are the best to use. Store in the crisper of the refrigerator without washing. Rinse as needed and use within two days. The leaves are excellent to use in salads, or to braise or cook as greens and serve as a vegetable dish.

The chicory root, dried, roasted, and ground, is used as a coffee substitute or additive to coffee. It adds aroma and body to the flavor. The French, Spanish, and Creoles are particularly fond of the chicory flavor in their coffee.

This herb heightens the flavor of many foods when added for seasoning. Use it in gravy, meat loaf, and dressing. (See *Herb, Vegetable* for additional information.)

CHIFFONADE *(shif′ uh nād′, -näd′)*—1. A garnish of finely cut herbs and vegetables used with soups and salads. 2. A salad dressing consisting of French dressing, chopped vegetables, and hard-cooked eggs.

Chiffonade Dressing

       ½ cup salad oil
       2 tablespoons vinegar
       2 tablespoons lemon juice
       2 teaspoons sugar
       ½ teaspoon dry mustard
       ½ teaspoon paprika
          Dash cayenne
       1 hard-cooked egg, chopped
       ¼ cup chopped cooked beets
       2 tablespoons snipped parsley
       1 tablespoon chopped onion

Combine salad oil, vinegar, lemon juice, sugar, ½ teaspoon salt, dry mustard, paprika, and cayenne in screw-top jar. Cover and shake. Add egg, beets, parsley, and onion; shake well. Chill. Shake again just before serving over vegetable salads. Makes 1 cup dressing.

CHIFFON CAKE—A light, rich cake made with salad oil instead of solid shortening. This was one of the first new types of cakes to be developed for centuries. Developed in 1949, it combines the richness of shortened cakes with the lightness of foam cakes. They are classified as foam cakes because there is no creaming of shortening and sugar and because stiffly beaten egg whites help to leaven the cake.

How to prepare: The basic method of making chiffon cake is quick and easy. The dry ingredients are sifted into a mixing bowl and a well is made in the center. Salad oil, egg yolks, liquids, and flavorings are poured into the well. Then the mixture is beaten into a smooth batter.

Egg whites are beaten in a second large bowl. The volume of the chiffon cake depends on beating the whites correctly. Be sure all utensils are free of grease. This will keep the whites from developing the volume that they should. Avoid using a plastic bowl which may retain a greasy film. Have the egg whites at room temperature so that a greater volume will be developed as they are beaten. Beat till very stiff peaks form—when a spatula is pulled through, a clear path should remain.

Pour the egg yolk batter in a thin stream over the entire surface of the egg whites. Fold gently into the egg whites. Use a rubber spatula with down-up-over motion, turning the bowl after each stroke. Always fold gently; never stir the batter.

The cake is baked in an ungreased pan. Ten-inch tube pans are normally used but small cakes can be baked in loaf or round cake pans. The cake is done if it springs back when pressed lightly with the finger.

Chiffon cake is turned upside-down to cool. This is necessary to keep the cake from shrinking or falling. When cool, loosen the cake around the sides and center tube with a metal spatula or knife and remove it from the pan.

How to frost: Chiffon cake may be frosted or left unfrosted, depending on personal preference and how it will be served.

The frostings used with chiffon cakes are usually light and fluffy. Seven-minute frosting, icings, and glazes are good to use.

Blend the flavors of maple, brown sugar, and walnuts with light-textured cake for an elegant dessert. Maple Chiffon Cake, decorated with tiny mums and grapes, highlights a fall meal.

Follow these rules for a perfect chiffon cake: Sift dry ingredients into bowl and make well in center. Add liquids in order listed. Beat smooth.

Beat egg whites till very stiff peaks form. Pour egg yolk batter in a thin stream over the whites, gently folding to blend. Bake in *ungreased* pan.

Invert tube pan to cool as soon as cake is baked. When cool, loosen sides with a spatula and turn upside down; remove pan. Frost, if desired.

In both texture and flavor, these light frostings suit the delicate foam cakes. The sturdy texture of chiffon cake can also support a butter frosting, but it is not suggested for other types of foam cakes.

Frosted chiffon cake is a flavorful, yet light, dessert or refreshment.

This cake, also, is rich enough to be served without a frosting. It's especially good with milk for snacks, to pack in lunch boxes, or to serve as a dessert at lunch or after a light supper. (See also *Cake*.)

Maple Chiffon Cake

    2¼ cups sifted cake flour
     ¾ cup granulated sugar
      3 teaspoons baking powder
      1 teaspoon salt
     ¾ cup brown sugar
          • • •
     ½ cup salad oil
      5 egg yolks
     ¾ cup cold water
      2 teaspoons maple flavoring
      1 cup egg whites (about 8)
     ½ teaspoon cream of tartar
      1 cup finely chopped walnuts
          • • •
     ½ cup butter or margarine
      4 cups sifted confectioners' sugar
      1 teaspoon vanilla *or* ½ to 1
          teaspoon maple flavoring
          Light cream (about ¼ cup)

Sift flour, granulated sugar, baking powder, and salt together into mixing bowl; stir in brown sugar. Make a well in center of dry ingredients. Add in order: salad oil, egg yolks, water, and flavoring. Beat till satin smooth.

Beat egg whites with cream of tartar till *very stiff peaks* form. Pour batter in thin stream over entire surface of egg whites; fold in gently. Fold in nuts. Bake in *ungreased* 10-inch tube pan at 350° for 1 hour. Invert pan; cool. Prepare frosting and frost cake.

For frosting: Melt butter or margarine in saucepan; keep over low heat till golden brown. Watch carefully to prevent scorching. Remove from heat. Place sifted confectioners' sugar in mixing bowl. Beat in melted butter. Add vanilla *or* maple flavoring. Blend in light cream till of spreading consistency.

Chocolate Chiffon Cake

      4 1-ounce squares unsweetened
          chocolate, melted
     ¼ cup sugar
    2¼ cups sifted cake flour
    1½ cups sugar
      3 teaspoons baking powder
     ½ cup salad oil
      7 egg yolks
      1 teaspoon vanilla
     ½ teaspoon cream of tartar
      7 egg whites

Thoroughly blend melted chocolate, ½ cup boiling water, and ¼ cup sugar; cool. Sift together flour, 1½ cups sugar, baking powder, and 1 teaspoon salt into bowl. Make well in center of dry ingredients. Add in order: salad oil, egg yolks, ¾ cup cold water, and vanilla. Beat till satin smooth. Stir in chocolate mixture.

In large mixing bowl combine cream of tartar and egg whites; beat till *very stiff peaks* form. Pour chocolate batter in thin stream over entire surface of egg whites; fold in gently. Bake in *ungreased* 10-inch tube pan at 325° for 1 hour and 5 minutes. Invert pan; cool.

Golden Chiffon Cake

    2¼ cups sifted cake flour
    1½ cups sugar
      3 teaspoons baking powder
     ½ cup salad oil
      5 egg yolks
     ¾ cup water
      1 teaspoon vanilla
      2 teaspoons grated lemon peel
     ½ teaspoon cream of tartar
      1 cup egg whites (about 8)

Sift together flour, sugar, baking powder, and 1 teaspoon salt into bowl. Make well in center. Add in order: salad oil, egg yolks, water, vanilla, and lemon peel. Beat till satin smooth.

Add cream of tartar to egg whites; beat till *very stiff peaks* form. Pour batter in thin stream over entire surface of egg whites; fold in gently. Bake in *ungreased* 10-inch tube pan at 325° for 1 hour and 10 minutes. Invert pan; cool. If desired, frost with seven-minute frosting tinted with a few drops yellow food coloring and sprinkle with tinted coconut.

Satisfy everyone's taste and fit any occasion with glamorous chiffon pies. This colorful array of pies includes Pumpkin Chiffon, Daiquiri Pie, Raspberry Chiffon, and Chocolate Chiffon.

CHIFFON PIE—A fluffy, delicate pie made of stiffly beaten egg whites or whipped cream, egg yolks, gelatin, and flavoring.

The name chiffon describes the very light texture which develops from folding in egg whites or whipped cream. The delicate filling is supported by the gelatin.

Many variations of chiffon pie are possible. The crusts may be either a baked pastry shell or a crumb crust. Filling flavors can range from chocolate, coffee, and rum to fruit. Fruit fillings use fresh or frozen fruits and juices. Garnishes can also be varied for interest and to fit the occasion. Whipped cream, chocolate curls, nut halves, twists of citrus fruits, or berries are attractive on chiffon pies.

The technique for making chiffon pies involves following a few simple rules. To make a smooth pie, it is important to have the gelatin at just the right consistency— partially set but still pourable. Partially set gelatin and flavorings are folded into stiffly beaten egg whites or whipped cream. To obtain a full, fluffy filling, this gelatin mixture is chilled until it mounds slightly, then piled into a baked and cooled pastry shell or crumb crust. The pie is chilled till firm—several hours or overnight—and garnished as desired just before serving.

Chiffon pies are best served well chilled. Because of their light texture, coolness, and richness, they are refreshing summer desserts, and they are especially good for ladies' luncheons or other social occasions. (See also *Pie*.)

Pumpkin Chiffon Pie

    1 envelope unflavored gelatin
   3/4 cup sugar
   1/2 teaspoon ground cinnamon
   1/2 teaspoon ground allspice
   1/4 teaspoon ground ginger
   1/4 teaspoon ground nutmeg
   3/4 cup milk
   2 slightly beaten egg yolks
   1 cup canned pumpkin
   2 egg whites
   1/2 cup whipping cream
   1 9-inch graham–cracker crust
     (See *Crumb Crust*)

In saucepan combine gelatin, 1/2 *cup* sugar, 1/2 teaspoon salt, cinnamon, allspice, ginger, and nutmeg. Stir in milk, egg yolks, and pumpkin. Cook and stir over medium heat till mixture boils and gelatin dissolves. Remove from heat and chill till partially set.

   Beat egg whites till soft peaks form; gradually add remaining sugar and beat to stiff peaks. Whip cream; fold into pumpkin with egg whites. Pile into crust. Chill till firm. Trim with whipped cream and walnuts, if desired.

Daiquiri Pie

  1 1/3 cups sugar
   1 envelope unflavored gelatin
   1/3 cup lime juice
   3 well–beaten egg yolks
   1/2 teaspoon grated lime peel
   2 drops green food coloring
   1/4 cup light rum
   3 egg whites
   1 9-inch *baked* pastry shell*

In medium saucepan, combine *1 cup* sugar, gelatin, and 1/4 teaspoon salt. Add lime juice and 1/3 cup water. Stir in egg yolks; mix well. Cook and stir over medium heat till mixture boils and gelatin dissolves. Remove from heat; stir in lime peel and food coloring. Cool to room temperature; stir in rum. Chill till partially set.

   Beat egg whites to soft peaks. Gradually add remaining sugar; beat to stiff peaks. Fold in gelatin mixture. Chill till mixture mounds. Pile into cooled shell. Chill till firm, 4 to 6 hours. Top Daiquiri Pie with whipped cream and candy lime slices, if desired.

Raspberry Chiffon Pie

Thaw and drain one 10-ounce package frozen red raspberries, reserving syrup. Add water to syrup to make 2/3 cup. Dissolve one 3-ounce package raspberry-flavored gelatin in 3/4 cup boiling water; add 2 tablespoons lemon juice and raspberry syrup. Chill, stirring occasionally, till partially set. Whip 1/2 cup whipping cream. Beat gelatin mixture till soft peaks form; fold in raspberries and whipped cream.

   Add dash salt to 2 egg whites; beat till soft peaks form. Add 1/4 cup sugar gradually; beat till stiff peaks form. Fold egg whites into raspberry mixture. Pile filling into one 9-inch *baked* pastry shell*, cooled. Chill till raspberry filling is firm. Garnish with additional whipped cream and raspberries, if desired.

Chocolate Chiffon Pie

   1 envelope unflavored gelatin
   3 egg yolks
   1/3 cup sugar
   1/4 teaspoon salt
   1 teaspoon vanilla
   2 1-ounce squares unsweetened
     chocolate
   1/2 cup water
   3 egg whites
   1/2 cup sugar
   1 9-inch *baked* pastry shell*
     Whipping cream (optional)

Soften gelatin in 1/4 cup cold water. Beat egg yolks till thick and lemon-colored. Gradually beat in the 1/3 cup sugar; add salt and vanilla. Combine chocolate and 1/2 cup water; stir over low heat till blended. Add softened gelatin; stir to dissolve. Immediately beat chocolate mixture into egg yolks. Chill, stirring occasionally, till mixture is partially set.

   Beat egg whites to soft peaks. Gradually add 1/2 cup sugar, beating to stiff peaks. Fold small amount of egg whites into chilled chocolate mixture. Then spoon about *half* the chocolate over remaining egg whites; fold in just till blended. Repeat with remaining chocolate. If necessary, chill till mixture mounds when spooned. Pile into cooled shell. Chill till firm. Whip cream and garnish with whipped cream and chocolate curls, if desired.

   *(See *Pastry* for recipe.)

CHILI, CHILE, CHILLI *(chil'ē)*—A very hot pepper of the *Capsicum* genus. They are the strongest of the *Capsicums*—the smallest peppers are the hottest.

Chilies, fresh or canned, have many recipe uses where their fiery touch lends just the right accent. They can be chopped and used in casseroles or dips or left whole and stuffed with cheese, then coated with a batter for a Mexican dish. Whole peppers can be pickled and served on a relish tray. (See also *Pepper*.)

Chilies Rellenos Con Queso

A favorite Mexican main dish, made with canned or fresh green chilies—

Cut 3 canned green peeled chilies in half cross-wise *or* use 3 fresh long green hot peppers. (To prepare fresh peppers, place on baking sheet in 450° oven till skins form black blisters, about 15 minutes, giving a quarter turn once. Peppers will be cooked. Cool slightly. Peel and carefully remove the stems and seeds; cut in half.) Stuff chilies with 4 to 6 ounces sharp natural Cheddar cheese, shredded (1 to 1½ cups). Coat the peppers with all-purpose flour.

Beat 6 egg whites till stiff, but not dry, peaks form. Add 3 tablespoons all-purpose flour and ¼ teaspoon salt to 6 egg yolks. Beat till thick and lemon-colored. Fold the egg yolk mixture into the beaten egg whites.

For each Chili Relleno, spoon about ⅓ cup of egg batter into ½-inch hot fat (375°) in skillet. Spread batter into a circle. As batter begins to set, gently top each mound with a cheese-stuffed chili. Cover with another ⅓ cup batter. Continue cooking till underside is browned, 2 to 3 minutes. Turn carefully; brown second side. Drain thoroughly on absorbent paper. Serve at once. Makes 6 servings.

CHILI CON CARNE—A dish originating in Mexico made with cubed or ground beef, chilies or chili powder, and usually, beans. The literal translation of the Spanish words is chili with meat.

Homemade chili is a popular dish for a cold day. It can also be purchased in cans with or without beans. Accompany with crisp relishes and crackers.

For Chilies Rellenos Con Queso, a cheese-stuffed chili pepper is set on a mound of egg batter that has been cooked in hot fat till set. Another mound of batter is then spooned over the pepper. When the underside has browned, it's carefully turned over.

Chili Con Carne

    1 pound ground beef
    1 cup chopped onion
    ¾ cup chopped green pepper
    1 16-ounce can tomatoes (2 cups),
        broken up
    1 16-ounce can dark red kidney
        beans (2 cups), drained
    1 8-ounce can tomato sauce
    1 teaspoon salt
    1 to 2 teaspoons chili powder
    1 bay leaf

In heavy skillet cook meat, onion, and green pepper till meat is browned and vegetables are tender. Stir in remaining ingredients. Cover; simmer 1 hour. Remove bay leaf. Serves 4.

Mexican favorites

Serve south-of-the-border specialties for →
dinner such as Chilies Rellenos Con Queso, Cheese Enchiladas (See *Enchilada* for recipe), and Mexican-Style Steak surrounding a mound of rice (See *Steak* for recipe).

CHILI POWDER—A blended spice containing ground, dried red chili peppers, ground cumin seed, ground oregano, and garlic powder. Ground cloves, ground allspice, or powdered onion are often added. No two manufacturers' blends are exactly alike.

This seasoning is an American invention. The basic blend we know today was developed by settlers in the Southwest.

Chili powder is used extensively when preparing Mexican-type foods. A dash adds flavor to main-dish recipes as well as to salads and appetizers. (See also *Spice.*)

Chili Cheese Log

    1 3-ounce package cream cheese
    8 ounces sharp process American
        cheese, shredded (2 cups)
    1 tablespoon lemon juice
    ¼ teaspoon garlic powder
        Dash red pepper
    ¼ cup finely chopped pecans
    1 teaspoon chili powder
    1 teaspoon paprika

Let cheeses stand till softened; combine with lemon, garlic, and red pepper. Beat till light and fluffy. Stir in nuts. Shape in roll 1½-inches across. Sprinkle with mixture of chili powder and paprika. Chill. Let stand at room temperature 10 minutes. Serve with crackers.

Chili–Bean Salad

    2 16-ounce cans green beans,
        drained and chilled
    ¾ cup diced celery
    ¼ cup small white onion rings
    2 tablespoons pickle relish
        Chili Salad Dressing

Combine beans, celery, onion rings, relish, and ½ teaspoon salt. Add Chili Salad Dressing; toss. Cover; chill 1 hour.

Chili Salad Dressing: In mixing bowl combine 2 tablespoons salad oil, ½ small clove garlic, ¼ teaspoon chili powder, ⅛ teaspoon salt, and dash pepper. Let stand 1 hour. Remove and discard garlic. Add 1 tablespoon vinegar and 1½ teaspoons lemon juice; beat with rotary beater. Chill thoroughly. Serves 6 to 8.

CHILI SAUCE—A relish made of tomatoes, onions, celery, sweet red or mild green peppers, and spices. Despite its name, chili sauce is not fiery hot in flavor. It resembles catsup, but it is not strained. Chili sauce can be purchased bottled, or prepared and canned at home. (See also *Sauce.*)

Chili Sauce

    1 peck tomatoes (12 to 14 pounds)
    1 pound celery (about 2 bunches),
        chopped (about 4 cups)
    1 quart small onions, ground
        (about 2½ cups)
    3 green peppers, ground
        (about 2½ cups)
        • • •
    6 inches stick cinnamon
    2 pounds brown sugar (4½ cups)
    1 quart cider vinegar
    1 tablespoon dry mustard
    1½ teaspoons ground cloves

Scald tomatoes; peel, core, and slice in chunks into large kettle. Cook 15 minutes; drain off *half* (about 6 cups) the juice (use for drinking or cooking). Add celery, onion, and green pepper; simmer about 1½ hours. Tie cinnamon in cloth; add with brown sugar, vinegar, mustard, cloves, and ¼ cup salt to tomato mixture.

Continue cooking 1½ hours. Remove cinnamon. Fill hot pint jars to within ½ inch of top; adjust lids. Process in boiling water bath 5 minutes (start timing when water returns to boil). Label jars. Makes 9 pints.

Chili–Cheese Mold

    1 envelope unflavored gelatin
        (1 tablespoon)
    1 cup chili sauce
    1 cup cream-style cottage cheese
    ½ cup mayonnaise
    ½ cup whipping cream

Soften gelatin in ¾ cup cold water; dissolve over low heat. Combine chili sauce, cottage cheese, mayonnaise, and ½ teaspoon salt; add gelatin. Whip cream; fold in. Turn into 1-quart mold. Chill till firm. Unmold on serving plate; pass an assortment of crackers.

CHILL—To cool food thoroughly, usually in the refrigerator at above-freezing temperature. Food may also be chilled with ice.

CHINESE ARTICHOKE—An herb with a tuber that is eaten as a vegetable. Sometimes this vegetable is referred to as the Japanese artichoke or knotroot.

The knotty, white tuber grows two to three inches long. Pick fresh, firm artichokes and avoid discolored or soft ones. The Chinese artichoke can be cleaned, then cooked or combined with a salad dressing to eat raw as a salad.

CHINESE CABBAGE—A vegetable belonging to the mustard family, often called celery cabbage. The thick, compact white stalks somewhat resemble celery and are topped with light green leaves. The flavor is cabbagelike, but more delicate, milder, and sweeter. Chinese cabbage adds a special flavor and crispness to salads and the quickly cooked Oriental dishes.

The Chinese cabbage called *bok choy* vaguely resembles celery. The stalks are white but not as compactly bunched, and the leaves are deep green and large. *Bok choy* is used in Oriental dishes.

This long slender head that looks like celery is called Chinese cabbage. It can be eaten raw or cooked as a vegetable.

Chop Chop Salad

1 medium head Chinese cabbage, thinly sliced (about 6 cups)
1½ cups cold cooked rice
1 10–ounce package frozen peas, cooked, drained, and cooled
2 cups diced cooked pork
1 5–ounce can water chestnuts, drained and sliced
½ cup mayonnaise
½ cup dairy sour cream
1 teaspoon celery seed
1 teaspoon monosodium glutamate

Toss together first 5 ingredients. Combine remaining ingredients and ½ teaspoon salt. Toss with salad. Chill till served. Makes about 6 main dish servings.

CHINESE COOKERY—A type of cooking that is often characterized by meticulous preparation and quick cooking of simple, attractive, well-blended mixtures. Fast cooking helps retain much of the original taste, color, and texture of the foods, particularly vegetables. It also produces the crisp-tender contrast in textures so characteristic of Chinese dishes.

Chinese cookery combines the ideas of four regional areas, each contributing to the national cuisine. Many of the dishes are simple, and the seasonings are uncomplicated. Chief seasonings are soy sauce, garlic, ginger, and sugar. Popular ingredients include rice, pork, chicken, duck, chicken stock, bamboo shoots, water chestnuts, Chinese cabbage, Chinese pea pods, and bean sprouts. Cornstarch is used to thicken sauces of many Chinese dishes, giving them a translucent appearance.

A basic piece of cooking equipment in Chinese cookery is the wok, a pan with a round bottom and sloping sides.

Chinese cuisine has become popular in both home-cooked meals and in restaurants. (See *Oriental Cookery, Wok* for additional information.)

CHINESE FIREPOT, MONGOLIAN FIREPOT—1. An Oriental main dish where guests cook their own food in broth at the table. 2. The name of the utensil used for cooking this Chinese dish. The cooker consists of a pan with a chimney through the center. The chimney is filled with charcoal which is lighted, keeping the broth in the pan simmering throughout the meal.

The food to be cooked can be cut, sliced, and arranged ahead of serving; the sauces to be used can be mixed and waiting. When guests are ready to eat, heat the broth in the pot and arrange the sauces and raw foods around the firepot. Each guest then uses chopsticks, bamboo tongs, long-handled forks, or wire ladles to pick up the desired food and holds or drops it into the simmering broth. Because the pieces of food are small, cooking takes a very short time. The guest removes his food and dips it into one of the sauces provided. After cooking is completed, eggs can be poached in the flavored broth and served to the guests. Otherwise, the final step is to dash some dry sherry into the broth and ladle it into small cups.

For dessert, try fruit, tea, and fortune cookies. (See also *Oriental Cookery*.)

Chinese Firepot

    ¾ pound large raw shrimp, peeled
        and cleaned (about 12 shrimp)
    2 uncooked chicken breasts,
        skinned, boned, and sliced
        very thin across grain
    ½ pound uncooked beef sirloin,
        sliced *very* thin across grain
    ½ head Chinese cabbage *or* 1 head-
        lettuce heart, coarsely cubed
    1 cup cubed eggplant *or* 1 5-ounce
        can water chestnuts, drained
        and sliced thin
 1½ cups halved fresh mushrooms
    4 cups small fresh spinach
        leaves, with stems removed
    6 13¾-ounce cans (10½ cups)
        or 2 46-ounce cans chicken
        broth (not condensed)*
    1 tablespoon grated gingerroot
        or 1 teaspoon ground ginger
      Chinese Mustard
      Ginger Soy
      Peanut Sauce
      Red Sauce
      Hot cooked rice

Shortly before cooking time, arrange raw meats and vegetables on large tray or platter and fill bowl with spinach. Provide chopsticks, bamboo tongs, long-handled forks, or wire ladles as cooking tools for guests.

In a firepot heat chicken broth and grated gingerroot or ground ginger to a gentle boil for cooking meat and vegetables. (An electric skillet, chafing dish, or fondue cooker* can be substituted for the firepot.)

Set out small bowls of the dunking sauces. Each guest picks up desired food with chopsticks or tongs and drops it into the bubbling broth. When tidbits are cooked, they lift them out and dip into sauce on plate. (Add more broth if needed.) Serve with rice. Serves 6.

*For fondue cooker, use two 13¾-ounce cans chicken broth and 1 teaspoon grated gingerroot or ¼ teaspoon ground ginger.

Chinese Mustard

Stir ¼ cup boiling water into ¼ cup dry mustard. Add ½ teaspoon salt, 1 tablespoon salad oil, and dash turmeric. Makes ⅓ cup sauce.

Ginger Soy

In a saucepan combine ½ cup soy sauce and 1½ teaspoons ground ginger. Bring to boiling. Serve hot or cold. Makes ½ cup.

Peanut Sauce

In a bowl thoroughly combine ¼ cup chunk-style peanut butter, 2 teaspoons soy sauce, 1½ teaspoons water, ¼ teaspoon sugar, 1 drop bottled hot pepper sauce, and ½ clove garlic, minced. Stir in ¼ cup water. Makes ½ cup.

Red Sauce

In bowl mix together 3 tablespoons catsup, 3 tablespoons chili sauce, 1½ tablespoons prepared horseradish, 1 teaspoon lemon juice, and dash bottled hot pepper sauce. Makes ½ cup.

CHINESE GOOSEBERRY — Another name for the small, brown, kiwi fruit, imported from New Zealand. The fruit is oval and about the size of a lemon. It makes a delightful addition to salads. (See also *Kiwi*.)

CHINESE NOODLES—Includes several varieties, each made from a different grain—wheat, rice, corn, peas—and used in Chinese dishes. In the northern part of China, wheat is grown as the staple instead of rice; therefore, noodles have become the staple in that area.

To the Chinese, noodles mean longevity, and they are often served at birthday celebrations. Chinese noodles are usually very long, although they come in a variety of shapes and sizes.

There are a wide variety of Chinese noodles. Cellophane noodles, which are transparent, gelatinous, and flavorless, take on the flavor of other ingredients in the recipe. Dried noodles, which are packaged like spaghetti, are cooked before using as an ingredient. Often the Chinese quick-fry the cooked noodles until they are crisp and brown. Fresh Chinese noodles are also available in some specialty shops. This fresh product should be tightly wrapped and kept chilled in the refrigerator until it is used.

Rice sticks resemble cellophane noodles, but they have a different texture. The squares of pressed or rolled dough used as the wrappers for Chinese egg roll or *won ton* are sometimes considered noodles. (See also *Noodles*.)

CHINESE ORANGE—A name sometimes given to the kumquat. (See also *Kumquat*.)

CHINESE PARSLEY—Another name for the fresh, green leaves of coriander, an Old World herb. The Spanish call it *cilantro*. It looks like parsley and is used by the Chinese mainly as a garnish for main dishes or in soups. Store in a plastic bag or in the crisper of the refrigerator.

CHINESE PEA PODS—A variety of peas with a thin, tender pod and tiny, underdeveloped green peas. As the name implies, the whole pea pod is eaten. They are also referred to by other names, such as snow peas, French peas, or podded sugar peas.

Chinese pea pods can be purchased fresh in some Chinese markets or frozen in most supermarkets. Fresh pea pods are perishable and should be refrigerated, then used as quickly as possible.

This vegetable requires very little cooking and should be crunchy when eaten. Chinese pea pods add an Oriental flair to the meal and can be served as a vegetable, added to salads, or combined with chicken for an elegant main dish.

Peas and Almonds

In skillet cook ¼ cup chopped green onion with tops in 1 tablespoon salad oil till tender but not brown. Add one 7-ounce package frozen Chinese pea pods, thawed, and one 3-ounce can sliced mushrooms, drained. Toss and cook the mixture over high heat 1 minute.

Dissolve 1 chicken bouillon cube in ¼ cup boiling water. Combine 1 teaspoon cornstarch and 1 teaspoon cold water. Stir bouillon and cornstarch mixture into peas. Cook, uncovered, over high heat till mixture thickens and bubbles. Toss, adding 2 tablespoons toasted slivered almonds. Makes 4 servings.

Chicken Breasts a la Vegetables

     3 large chicken breasts, halved
     ⅓ cup all-purpose flour
     ¼ cup salad oil
     ¾ cup coarsely chopped onion
     ½ cup sliced celery
     1 clove garlic, minced
     1 10½-ounce can condensed cream
        of mushroom soup
     ¼ cup dry sherry
     1 6-ounce can sliced mushrooms,
        drained (about 1 cup)
     1 5-ounce can water chestnuts,
        drained and thinly sliced
     1 7-ounce package frozen Chinese
        pea pods, thawed

Coat chicken with flour; sprinkle with salt and pepper. Brown in hot salad oil in skillet. Remove chicken from skillet.

In same skillet cook onion, celery, and garlic till just tender. Blend in soup and wine. Add mushrooms and water chestnuts. Bring to boiling. Return chicken to skillet. Cover; simmer 20 minutes. Add pea pods; cover and simmer 10 minutes more. To serve, spoon some of the sauce over chicken. Pass remaining sauce. Makes 6 servings.

Chinese pea pods add a special crunch to main dishes, such as beef tenderloin-vegetable mixture—fit for company. They are often used in Oriental recipes using the stir-fry technique. (See also *Pea*.)

Chinese Beef Skillet

    1 7-ounce package frozen Chinese
        pea pods
    2 tablespoons salad oil
    1 pound beef tenderloin tips,
        sliced paper-thin across
        grain
    • • •
    1 tablespoon salad oil
    ¼ cup chopped onion
    1 small clove garlic, minced
    4 cups thinly sliced raw
        cauliflowerets (1 medium head)
    1 10½-ounce can condensed beef
        broth
    • • •
    2 tablespoons cornstarch
    ¼ cup soy sauce
        Hot cooked rice

Pour boiling water over frozen pea pods and carefully break apart with fork; drain.

Heat 2 tablespoons salad oil in skillet. Add *half* the beef and cook quickly, turning it over and over just till browned, about 1 or 2 minutes. Remove meat at once. Repeat with remaining beef in hot skillet. Remove beef.

Add 1 tablespoon salad oil to skillet and cook onion and garlic just a few seconds. Add cauliflower. Pour broth over and cook till cauliflower is crisp-cooked, about 3 minutes, stirring gently.

Mix cornstarch, soy sauce, and ¾ cup cold water till smooth. Stir into mixture in skillet. Add beef and pea pods. Cook, stirring constantly, till sauce thickens. Serve over rice. Pass additional soy sauce. Makes 6 servings.

CHIPOLATA *(chip uh läd' uh)*—A small, chive-flavored, spicy sausage.

CHIPPED BEEF—Lean beef that is pickled, then smoked and dried. It is usually prepared from the top round and sliced paper thin. Chipped beef is another name for dried beef. (See also *Dried Beef*.)

CHIP—The term used to describe irregular bits of food chopped from a larger piece or wafer-thin slices cut from some fruits or vegetables, such as potatoes, turnips, carrots, squash, or bananas. These thin slices are deep-fried until very crisp.

CHITTERLINGS, CHITLINGS *(chit' uhr - lings, chit' lins)*—The thoroughly cleaned, cooked intestines of a pig used in some regional dishes, especially in the South. Chitterlings are usually boiled and may be coated with cornmeal and fried after they are boiled. (See *Afro-American Cookery, Variety Meat* for additional information.)

CHIVE—A seasoning belonging to the onion family. It is a perennial plant grown as an herb and often used for ornamental purposes in the garden because of its tiny, colorful, lavender flowers.

This plant has been in existence for several thousand years and is native to some parts of North America, Europe, and Asia.

The part of the plant most often used in cooking is the slender, young, tender, dark green, tubular leaves. These leaves grow back when cut, just like grass; the purple flowers won't grow if the chives are constantly being cut. Sometimes the small, flat bulb part of the plant is used.

Chives are available in several different forms and can be enjoyed all year-round. Purchase a pot of fresh chives at the market, and you can enjoy the touch of color it adds to your kitchen. When buying a chive plant, look for fresh, bright green leaves, tender and crisp. Some hints to help chive plants grow: keep them in a sunny part of the kitchen; water frequently; snip often to within two or three inches of the base. A pair of scissors makes cutting up chives easy work.

If plant growing isn't a favorite hobby, frozen chives are available at most supermarkets. They are cleaned, chopped, and come packaged in plastic cartons. Store these chives in the freezer in the original carton. To use, loosen top layer with fork and remove the amount needed.

Chives also come freeze-dried. They are cleaned, chopped, and flash-frozen, then dehydrated and packaged. Look for this item on the herb and spice shelves in the

Add the springlike flavor of chives whenever a mild onion flavor is desired. They make a colorful trim for soups, too.

supermarket and store it on your own herb and spice shelf. Freeze-dried chives will be rehydrated by the liquid in any dish in which they are used.

Fresh, frozen, or dried chives can be used interchangeably in almost any recipe —in cooked foods, add the chives at the last minute, if possible, for best flavor.

Chives' mild onion flavor can be used effectively with cheese and egg dishes and similar light or delicate items. They add distinctive flavor to sauces, salads, salad dressings, soups, breads, and vegetables, and are delicious in dips. Chives are also one of the ingredients in the classic seasonings, *fines herbs*. (See also *Onion*.)

Chive Mayonnaise

   1 cup mayonnaise
  1/4 cup snipped chives
   1 tablespoon lemon juice
   2 teaspoons tarragon vinegar

Mix all ingredients and dash salt together. Serve with cooked fish fillets or steaks.

Chive Butter

Mix together 1/2 cup butter or margarine, softened; 1 tablespoon snipped chives; 1 tablespoon snipped parsley; 1/2 teaspoon dried tarragon leaves, crushed; and 1/2 teaspoon dried chervil leaves, crushed. Spread the chive butter on French bread slices. Wrap in foil and heat at 400° about 10 minutes. Or use on hot corn muffins, biscuits, or vegetables.

Chive and Corn Spoonbread

   2 cups milk
  3/4 cup yellow cornmeal
   2 tablespoons butter or margarine
   1 teaspoon salt
   4 egg yolks
   1 8-ounce can whole kernel corn
      (1 cup), drained
   3 tablespoons snipped chives
   4 stiffly beaten egg whites
     Butter or margarine

In saucepan scald milk; stir in cornmeal. Cook and stir till thickened. Remove from heat; stir in 2 tablespoons butter and the salt. Set aside to cool slightly.

Beat egg yolks, one at a time, into slightly cooled cornmeal mixture. Fold in corn, chives, and beaten egg whites. Turn into greased 10x6x1 1/2-inch baking dish. Bake at 350° till golden brown, about 35 to 40 minutes. Serve with butter. Makes 6 servings.

Swiss Potato Salad

   4 cups cubed, peeled, cooked
     potatoes
   1 teaspoon salt
   4 slices Swiss cheese (4 ounces),
     cut in narrow strips
   1 cup dairy sour cream
   3 tablespoons milk
   2 tablespoons snipped chives
  1/2 teaspoon dry mustard

Sprinkle potatoes with salt; combine with cheese strips. In small bowl blend together sour cream, milk, chives, and mustard; pour over potato mixture. Toss lightly. Serve at room temperature. Makes 4 or 5 servings.

CHOCOLATE

The many forms available prove its popularity as a food and versatility as a cooking ingredient.

Chocolate is a versatile food made from the bean of the cacao tree. It is the name of a beverage made with chocolate and water or milk, and the name given by many to candy having a chocolate coating.

The origin of the words chocolate and cacao is as interesting as their uses. Both words come from the Aztec language. Cacao is derived from *cacahuatl*, the name of the cacao bean, and chocolate stems from *chocólatl*, the name of a beverage. In 1720 a Swedish botanist gave the cacao tree its botanical name *Theobroma cacao*, which means cacao, food of the gods.

Cacao trees were originally grown in Central America and parts of South America. One legend attributes their discovery to a thirsty Aztec who started sucking the juicy pulp around the seed in the cacao pod. When his thirst was quenched, he threw some of the seeds into the fire. Soon the fire was giving off a spicy aroma. His curiosity aroused, he tasted the roasted bean and decided he liked it.

Some authorities believe the cacao beans were grown in the Western Hemisphere more than 3,000 years before the Spanish first arrived there and were used by the Indians as food and money.

Whatever the original use of the bean, when Cortez landed in Mexico around 1519, he was treated to the delicacy, *chocólatl*—the cold, bitter, syrupy beverage—by Montezuma, who was the emperor of the Aztecs at that time.

For an everyday or special occasion

← Semisweet chocolate in cake and unsweetened chocolate in frosting make Velvety Fudge Cake a double chocolate dessert.

The Spanish observed how this *chocólatl* was prepared and noted that the bean first was roasted and ground; then peppers, spices, and herbs were added. Later, the Spanish planted cacao trees in their New World colonies. When they decided to improve upon the beverage, *chocólatl*, they added sugar, vanilla, and cinnamon, and served it as a hot drink.

For nearly a century, the Spanish kept the production of chocolate a secret. Finally, the monopoly was broken. Some say that Spanish monks shared the secret with other monks in Italy. Others say that the use of the chocolate beverage in royal courts began its distribution across the Continent. And still others say it was after the marriage of a Spanish princess to Louis XIV that the French started using it.

In the mid-1600's chocolate-serving clubs sprang up all over Europe. Chocolate became a fashionable drink, probably because it was so expensive and only the rich could afford it. The cost was high because the beans were imported and because processing was done entirely by hand. Nevertheless, chocolate was in demand.

During the eighteenth century, a method for mass-producing chocolate was developed, and the price of chocolate dropped. No longer was the drink strictly for the wealthy people.

Chocolate was brought to America by New England traders. The first chocolate factory was built in New England near Dorchester, Massachusetts, in 1765. In 1828, the cocoa press—used to extract the cocoa butter—was invented. It made possible the development of molded bars for eating. In 1876 a Swiss invented a way of making milk chocolate. Later, a smooth fondant chocolate was developed to replace the earlier coarse-grained chocolate.

Unsweetened chocolate, also called bitter, cooking, or baking chocolate, comes in two forms—solid and semiliquid. The latter form needs no melting. These products, along with all chocolate products, come from cacao beans, which are shown at lower left.

Sweet chocolate is not only perfect for desserts, but delicious to eat as is. It comes in bars that are divided in sections, making it easy to separate if the recipe calls for part of the bar. Sometimes it's referred to as sweet cooking chocolate.

Semisweet chocolate pieces are just right for nibbling or cooking. They also can be purchased flavored with mint. This type is a little less sweet than sweet chocolate and also comes in bars or squares. The squares are used for chocolate-dipped candies.

Milk chocolate is used most often for eating and can be purchased in bar form, with or without nuts; in pieces; as candies; or in chunks. This lighter-colored chocolate has a milder flavor and can be used for desserts or melted as an ice cream topper.

How chocolate is produced: Cacao trees grow in tropical climates, in those countries near the equator. Some of the top growers are in West Africa, Brazil, Ecuador, Venezuela, and the Dominican Republic. In most cocoa-growing areas, the main harvest lasts for several months. Differences in climate can cause wide variation in harvest times from year to year, even in the same locations.

Cacao beans are about the size of almonds, and about 25 to 40 beans or seeds are embedded in the moist pulp inside a pod. The cacao tree is an evergreen, and pink, yellow, or white flowers grow in clusters on the trunk and main branches. The average cacao tree produces 20 to 30 pods in a year, each pod producing 1½ to 2 ounces of dried beans.

When ripe, the pods are cut from the trees by hand. They are then cut open and the seeds are scooped out. The next step is a fermenting process, necessary for flavor development. During this time the white, moist pulp disappears. The seeds are then dried in the sun or by artificial means before proceeding with next step.

To make chocolate, these dried beans are cleaned, weighed, blended, and then roasted to bring out their characteristic aroma. Next the beans are broken into little pieces, called nibs, and are separated from their outer shells. These nibs are more than 50 percent cocoa butter—an unusual vegetable fat. (Cocoa butter is a good keeper as it resists rancidity and is very stable.) This cocoa butter is liquefied and released by grinding, thus forming a chocolate liquor. This chocolate liquor is the basic substance in all forms of chocolate. The processing then continues, forming one of the following types—unsweetened chocolate, cocoa, sweet chocolate, milk chocolate, and semisweet chocolate.

Nutritional value: Chocolate is a source of fat and calories. One 1-ounce square unsweetened chocolate equals 142 calories; one 1-ounce square sweet chocolate, 133 calories; 1 tablespoon cocoa powder, 21 calories; 1 cup chocolate milk, 208 calories; 2 tablespoons chocolate sauce, 87 calories; and one 2x3x2-inch piece unfrosted devil's food cake, 165 calories.

Chocolate is a good source of quick, extra energy due to its easy digestibility. It has been taken along on many expeditions —to the tops of mountains, to the poles of the earth, as well as on space projects. Chocolate is one of the foods that is also included in survival kits for soldiers.

Types of chocolate

Chocolate is available in several different forms, all of which need to be stored in a cool, dry place at a temperature less than 75°. At higher temperatures, the cocoa butter in the chocolate begins to soften and rise to the surface. Upon cooling, the coating takes on a misty gray cast known as "bloom." This will not affect the flavor, nor does it mean the chocolate is undesirable. When the chocolate is melted, it will regain its original color.

For best results always use the kind of chocolate called for in a recipe. Ingredients are balanced, particularly in baked foods, to bring out the most desirable flavor.

Unsweetened chocolate: When the refined chocolate liquor is poured into molds and allowed to cool, small, hardened squares form. These one-ounce squares are individually paper-wrapped and, most often, are used melted in baking and cooking. This product is known as bitter, baking, or cooking chocolate. Larger, 10-pound blocks of the unsweetened chocolate are also formed for commercial use.

Another unsweetened baking product is made of cocoa and cocoa butter or vegetable fats in a semiliquid form, needing no melting before use. The one-ounce envelope or packet equals one ounce of melted unsweetened chocolate and is referred to as no-melt unsweetened chocolate. It is ready to use as purchased.

Sweet chocolate: To make this kind of chocolate, sugar and additional cocoa butter are added to unsweetened chocolate. These ingredients are then blended together to make a smooth paste. In some blends, vanilla, mint, or other flavorings are included. The sweet chocolate is molded, cooled, and hardened into sectioned bars for use in cooking or for eating.

Semisweet chocolate: The processing is the same as for sweet chocolate, except that less sugar is added. It is available packaged in bars, squares, or in pieces. These pieces are processed so that they will melt easily in cooking or hold their shape during baking at moderate oven temperatures. Semisweet chocolate is also used for eating; and, purchased in paper-wrapped squares, it is often used as a dipping chocolate or for making various kinds of candy.

Milk chocolate: This kind of chocolate is made with chocolate liquor, sugar, additional cocoa butter, and milk or cream. Vanilla is sometimes added for flavor. These ingredients are blended together, then molded into various forms. Milk chocolate is available in bar form, in pieces, like semisweet chocolate, and as candies or chunks. Sometimes nuts, raisins, coconut, or other ingredients are included.

Cocoa: Cocoa is another product made from the chocolate liquor. Part of the cocoa butter is removed and the remaining product is ground and sieved to a fine powder. It is available as regular and Dutch-process cocoa. Both are unsweetened products. Ready-to-use cocoa products are also available, and these contain sweetening and other flavorings. (See also *Cocoa.*)

Uses of chocolate

The cooking uses for chocolate are inexhaustible since its flavor is such a universal favorite. Chocolate is most commonly used in beverages and desserts and candies of all types. Sometimes it remains in pieces in the finished product; at other times it melts during the cooking process. To use chocolate effectively in many recipes, however, it must first be melted.

Extra care should be used when melting chocolate for use in a recipe to preserve its flavor. Because chocolate burns or scorches very easily—and develops an unpleasant flavor—it is important to remember that low heat must be used for melting any type of chocolate. Also, if it is heated too quickly, the chocolate may not melt smoothly and may produce a grainy, undesirable product.

Heat chocolate over hot, but not boiling, water until partially melted. Remove from heat and stir until smooth. Or, in a saucepan, heat the chocolate over a very low direct heat, stirring constantly.

Avoid adding a very small amount of moisture—a little steam, a bit of flavoring, or a bit of moisture—to the chocolate. This can cause the chocolate to stiffen or "tighten." Should this happen, the chocolate is not ruined. Revive it by stirring in a little vegetable shortening—not butter or margarine, for they contain a small amount of moisture. While a very small amount of liquid adversely affects melted chocolate, it can nevertheless be melted in the larger amounts of liquid called for in recipe ingredients.

Occasionally an emergency substitution of ingredients has to be made. Cocoa with the addition of fat can be substituted for unsweetened chocolate. The substitution is 3 tablespoons unsweetened cocoa powder plus 1 tablespoon fat equals one 1-ounce square of unsweetened chocolate.

As a beverage: Hot beverages made with chocolate are sure to be popular with the young crowd as a snack after school.

With the addition of coffee, a chocolate drink is turned into a mocha beverage, an adult favorite.

After Dinner Mocha

 1½ **cups water**
  ¼ **cup instant coffee powder**
  3 **tablespoons sugar**
  1 **1-ounce square unsweetened**
    chocolate
  3 **cups milk**
   Whipped cream
   Sugar

In saucepan combine water, coffee powder, 3 tablespoons sugar, chocolate, and dash salt. Stir over low heat till chocolate melts. Simmer 4 to 5 minutes, stirring constantly. Gradually add milk. Heat and stir till hot. Remove from heat and beat with rotary beater till frothy. Pour into cups. Spoon dollop of whipped cream on each. Pass extra sugar and whipped cream. Makes 3 or 4 servings.

Mexican Chocolate

  4 cups milk
  5 1-ounce squares semisweet
      chocolate, broken up
  6 inches stick cinnamon
  1 teaspoon vanilla

In saucepan combine milk, chocolate, and cinnamon. Cook over medium heat, stirring constantly, till chocolate melts and mixture is heated. Remove from heat; add vanilla.

Remove cinnamon sticks. Beat mixture vigorously with *molinillo* or rotary beater. Serve in warmed mugs. Makes 4 servings.

Beating Mexican Chocolate with an authentic *molinillo*, Mexican handmill, gives this chocolate beverage a foamy crown.

Hot Chocolate

  2 1-ounce squares unsweetened
      chocolate
  ¼ cup sugar
      Dash salt
  1 cup water
  4 cups milk

Combine chocolate, sugar, salt, and water in saucepan. Stir over low heat till chocolate melts. Gradually stir in milk; heat slowly just to boiling. Beat with rotary beater. Serve in heated cups. Makes 5 cups.

As a dessert or candy: If the last part of the meal or the between-meal snack is flavored with chocolate—whether it be a frozen chocolate dessert, a dessert from the oven, a velvety cake, a cookie or candy, or a creamy pie—it is almost guaranteed to be a huge success.

The frozen dessert can be as exciting as a chocolate chip ice cream flavored with molasses or a dessert from the freezer made with chocolate candy bars. Or, the baked dessert may be a puffy chocolate soufflé served with a sauce or a variation of an old-fashioned bread pudding.

Choco-Mo Ice Cream

Molasses ice cream with chocolate chips—

Combine 1 tablespoon cornstarch and ⅔ cup water in a saucepan. Stir in one 14½-ounce can evaporated milk (1⅔ cups). Cook and stir till mixture boils. Beat 3 egg yolks till light. Stir small amount of the hot mixture into egg yolks. Return to remaining hot mixture in saucepan. Cook and stir till mixture is almost boiling. Stir in ¼ cup light molasses and dash salt; chill the mixture in the refrigerator.

Beat 3 egg whites till soft peaks form. Gradually add ¼ cup sugar, beating till stiff peaks form. Fold into molasses mixture.

Turn into 11x7x1½-inch pan. Freeze till firm. Break in chunks and place in bowl; beat till smooth with electric mixer. Fold in ½ cup semisweet chocolate pieces that have been finely chopped. Return to cold pan. Freeze till firm. Makes 8 to 10 servings.

Several different chocolate products are used in these two delightful recipes, Coffee Toffee Squares and Brazilian Chocolate.

Coffee Toffee Squares

    1 cup chocolate wafer crumbs
    2 tablespoons butter or
        margarine, melted

    · · ·

    ½ cup butter or margarine
    ½ cup sugar
    4 egg yolks
    1 1-ounce square unsweetened
        chocolate, melted and cooled
    2 teaspoons instant coffee powder
    ½ teaspoon vanilla
    4 egg whites
    ¼ cup sugar
    3 ¾-ounce chocolate-covered
        toffee bars

For crust combine crumbs and 2 tablespoons melted butter or margarine. Press into bottom of 8x8x2-inch baking pan.

Cream together ½ cup butter and ½ cup sugar till light and fluffy. Thoroughly beat in egg yolks, chocolate, coffee powder, and vanilla.

Beat egg whites till soft peaks form. Gradually add ¼ cup sugar, beating till stiff peaks form. Fold egg white mixture into chocolate mixture. Spread over crust.

Coarsely crush toffee bars. Sprinkle over chocolate mixture. Freeze till firm, 3 to 4 hours. Makes 6 to 8 servings.

Chocolate Marble Squares

    1 cup vanilla wafer crumbs
    2 tablespoons butter, melted
    ½ cup butter or margarine
    1 4½-ounce milk chocolate candy
        bar
    4 beaten egg yolks
    ¼ cup sifted confectioners' sugar
    ½ cup slivered almonds, toasted
    4 stiffly beaten egg whites
    1 pint vanilla ice cream, softened

Combine crumbs and 2 tablespoons melted butter; press into bottom of 9x9x2-inch baking pan.

In saucepan melt ½ cup butter and candy bar over low heat. Cook and stir till blended. Stir small amount of hot mixture into egg yolks; return to saucepan. Cook and stir over low heat till thickened. Remove from heat. Add confectioners' sugar. Beat till smooth. Stir in *half* the toasted, slivered almonds; cool.

Fold into egg whites. Spoon over crust alternately with ice cream. Gently cut through to marble. Freeze till firm, about 6 hours. Cut in squares; sprinkle with remaining nuts. If desired, top with dollops of whipped cream, then sprinkle with nuts. Makes 9 servings.

Chocolate Soufflé

In saucepan blend ⅓ cup light cream and one 3-ounce package cream cheese over very low heat. Add ½ cup semisweet chocolate pieces. Cook and stir to melt chocolate; cool.

Beat 3 egg yolks with dash salt till thick and lemon-colored, about 5 minutes. Slowly blend into cooled chocolate.

Beat 3 egg whites to soft peaks. Gradually add ¼ cup sifted confectioners' sugar, beating to stiff peaks. Fold small amount of whites into chocolate mixture. Fold chocolate, half at a time, into the stiffly beaten egg whites. Pour mixture into an *ungreased* 1-quart soufflé dish.

Bake at 300° till a knife inserted halfway between center and edge comes out clean, about 50 minutes. Serve at once with Custard Sauce. Makes 5 or 6 servings.

Custard Sauce: Mix 4 beaten egg yolks, dash salt, and ¼ cup sugar in heavy saucepan. Gradually stir in 2 cups milk, scalded and slightly cooled. Cook and stir over low heat till mixture coats a metal spoon. Remove from heat. Cool pan at once in cold water. Stir a minute or two. Add 1 teaspoon vanilla. Chill.

Chocolate Meringue Pudding

A different version of bread pudding—

> 2 cups milk
> 1½ 1-ounce squares unsweetened chocolate
> 3 cups 1-inch day-old bread cubes
> ¼ cup brown sugar
> 1 teaspoon vanilla
> 2 beaten egg yolks
> 2 egg whites
> 3 tablespoons granulated sugar
> ½ teaspoon shredded orange peel

Combine milk and chocolate in saucepan. Cook and stir over low heat till chocolate melts. Place bread in bowl; pour chocolate mixture over. Add brown sugar, vanilla, egg yolks, and ¼ teaspoon salt. Mix lightly to blend.

Lightly grease six 5-ounce custard cups. Set in shallow baking pan and fill with pudding mixture. Pour hot water 1-inch deep around cups. Bake at 350° till knife inserted comes out clean, about 30 to 35 minutes.

Meanwhile, prepare meringue. In mixing bowl beat egg whites till soft peaks form. Gradually add granulated sugar, beating till stiff peaks form. Fold in shredded orange peel. Remove puddings from oven. Add a dollop of meringue. Bake till meringue is lightly browned, about 10 minutes. Makes 6 servings.

Chocolate also is a favorite for use in cakes and frostings. Who can resist a luscious, velvety wedge of cake topped with chocolate frosting? The chocolate cake will appear more red if baking soda is used as the leavening agent, although too much soda will give an undesirable flavor.

Velvety Fudge Cake

This one is made with semisweet chocolate—

> 1 6-ounce package semisweet chocolate pieces (1 cup)
> ¼ cup butter or margarine
> ¾ cup sugar
> 1 teaspoon vanilla
> 2 eggs
> 1½ cups sifted all-purpose flour
> ¾ teaspoon baking soda
> 1 cup sour milk *or* buttermilk
> Creamy Chocolate Frosting

In small saucepan melt chocolate over very low heat, stirring constantly; cool. Thoroughly cream together butter or margarine, sugar, and vanilla. Stir in melted chocolate. Add eggs, one at a time, beating well after each. Sift together flour, baking soda, and ½ teaspoon salt. Add dry ingredients to creamed mixture alternately with sour milk *or* buttermilk, beating the mixture well after each addition.

Pour into 2 greased and floured 8x1½-inch round cake pans. Bake at 350° till done, about 25 to 30 minutes. Frost.

Creamy Chocolate Frosting: In small saucepan melt two 1-ounce squares unsweetened chocolate over low heat; cool. Beat together one 3-ounce package softened cream cheese and 2 tablespoons milk. Add 2 cups sifted confectioners' sugar; mix well. Beat in the melted chocolate, another 2 tablespoons milk, and 1½ teaspoons vanilla. Add enough additional sifted confectioners' sugar (about 2½ to 2¾ cups) to make frosting of spreading consistency.

Chocolate Layer Cake

In mixing bowl cream ⅔ cup butter or margarine. Gradually add 1¾ cups sugar, creaming till mixture is light. Add 1 teaspoon vanilla and 2 eggs, one at a time, beating well after each. Blend in 2½ 1-ounce squares unsweeteneed chocolate, melted and cooled.

Sift together 2½ cups sifted cake flour, 1¼ teaspoons baking soda, and ½ teaspoon salt. Add to creamed mixture alternately with 1¼ cups icy cold water, beating after each addition. Pour into 2 greased and floured 9x1½-inch round cake pans. Bake at 350° till done, about 30 to 35 minutes. Frost.

Sweet Chocolate Cake

    1 4-ounce bar sweet cooking
       chocolate
  ⅓ cup water
  ½ cup butter or margarine
    1 cup sugar
    3 egg yolks
    1 teaspoon vanilla
      . . .
1¾ cups sifted cake flour
    1 teaspoon baking soda
  ½ teaspoon salt
  ⅔ cup buttermilk
    3 egg whites
      Coconut Frosting

Combine chocolate and water in saucepan. Stir over low heat till chocolate melts. Cool.

Cream butter or margarine; gradually add sugar, creaming till light. Add egg yolks, one at a time, beating well after each. Blend in vanilla and chocolate mixture.

Sift together flour, baking soda, and salt. Add to creamed mixture alternately with buttermilk, beating after each addition. Beat egg whites to stiff peaks. Fold into batter. Pour into 2 greased and lightly floured 8x1½-inch round cake pans. Bake at 350° for 30 to 35 minutes. Cool. Spread Coconut Frosting between layers and on top of the cake.

Coconut Frosting: Combine one 6-ounce can evaporated milk (⅔ cup), ⅔ cup sugar, ¼ cup butter or margarine, 1 slightly beaten egg, and dash salt. Cook and stir over medium heat till mixture thickens and bubbles, about 12 minutes. Cool slightly. Add 1 teaspoon vanilla, 1⅓ cups flaked coconut, and ½ cup chopped pecans; mix well. Cool.

Choco-Blender Frosting

Put 1 cup sugar in blender container; cover and blend at high speed about 1 minute. Add three 1-ounce squares unsweetened chocolate, cut in small pieces; one 6-ounce can evaporated milk (⅔ cup); and dash salt. Blend at high speed of blender till frosting is thick enough for spreading consistency, about 3 minutes.

If necessary, use rubber spatula to scrape sides of blender container. Makes enough to frost the tops of two 8-inch layers. (If firmer frosting is desired, chill frosted cake.)

Fill the cookie jar or candy dish with freshly made chocolate treats and watch them disappear. Cookies and candies can serve as an energy booster between meals or for dessert to satisfy a sweet tooth. Bar cookies, in particular, make good take-along desserts for lunch boxes.

Chocolate Chippers

  ½ cup shortening
  ½ cup granulated sugar
  ¼ cup brown sugar
    1 egg
    1 teaspoon vanilla
    1 cup sifted all-purpose flour
  ½ teaspoon baking soda
  ¾ teaspoon salt
    1 6-ounce package semisweet
      chocolate pieces (1 cup)
  ½ cup chopped walnuts

Cream shortening, sugars, egg, and vanilla till fluffy. Sift together flour, baking soda, and salt; stir into creamed mixture.

Stir in chocolate pieces and chopped walnuts. Drop from teaspoon 2 inches apart onto greased cookie sheet. Bake at 375° for 10 to 12 minutes. Remove from pan. Makes 3 dozen.

Double Chocolate Bars

Cream ¼ cup butter or margarine, ¾ cup sugar, and 1 teaspoon vanilla till fluffy. Add ¼ cup light corn syrup and continue creaming. Beat in 2 eggs and two 1-ounce squares unsweetened chocolate, melted and cooled.

Sift together 1 cup sifted all-purpose flour, ½ teaspoon salt, and ½ teaspoon baking powder. Stir into batter. Fold in one-half 6-ounce package semisweet chocolate pieces (½ cup) and ½ cup chopped walnuts. Spread in greased 9x9x2-inch baking pan. Bake at 350° for 25 minutes. Cut in bars when cool.

The all-American favorite

Mint-flavored semisweet chocolate can be →
substituted in Chocolate Chippers for a new and different flavor sensation.

Chocolate Swirl Cookies

½ cup butter or margarine
1 cup sugar
2 eggs
2 1-ounce squares unsweetened
    chocolate, melted
1 teaspoon vanilla

. . .

2 cups sifted all-purpose flour
1½ teaspoons baking powder
½ teaspoon salt
½ teaspoon baking soda
½ teaspoon ground cinnamon
¼ teaspoon ground ginger
¼ teaspoon ground allspice
    Sugar

Cream butter and 1 cup sugar till light and fluffy. Add eggs, chocolate, and vanilla; beat well. Sift together next 7 ingredients; stir into creamed mixture. Blend well. Chill.

To form swirls roll about 2 teaspoons cookie dough on lightly floured board with hands to form a rope about 9 inches long. Carefully place on cookie sheet and coil into spiral shape. Sprinkle with sugar. Bake at 350° for 10 minutes. Makes about 5 dozen.

Chocolate Cherries

Drain one 8-ounce jar whole maraschino cherries thoroughly on paper toweling. Prepare one 12-ounce package chocolate fudge mix according to package directions, *except* leave mixture over simmering water after it becomes glossy. Using fork, dip each cherry into fudge mixture, turning to coat evenly. Push onto waxed paper with another fork. Stir fudge mixture frequently. Pour remaining fudge into a small buttered pan. Makes 2½ dozen.

Note: These will not freeze or store well.

Chocolate pies are always appreciated and enjoyed, whether they get a quick head start with convenience products, such as pudding or dessert mixes, or are made from scratch.

To trim the tops of pies or cakes with chocolate curls, use a 4-ounce bar of sweet cooking chocolate at room temperature. Using a vegetable peeler, carefully shave off thin slices of the chocolate and watch it curl as it is being cut. The temperature of the chocolate is very important—if too cold, the chocolate curls will break. If the chocolate is breaking into shreds as it is being cut, it may help to dip the vegetable peeler in warm water.

Chocolate-Flecked Chiffon Pie

1 envelope unflavored gelatin
1 cup sugar
1 cup milk
2 1-ounce squares unsweetened
    chocolate
2 2-ounce packages dessert topping
    mix *or* 2 cups whipping cream
1 *baked* 9-inch pastry shell
    (See *Pastry*)

Combine gelatin, sugar, and dash salt in saucepan. Add milk; cut chocolate in small pieces and add. Cook and stir over medium heat till gelatin is dissolved and chocolate is melted. (Mixture will be chocolate flecked.) Chill, stirring occasionally, till mixture mounds.

Prepare dessert topping mix according to package directions or whip cream. Fold into gelatin mixture. Pile into cooled pastry shell. Chill till firm. If desired, trim with additional whipped cream and chocolate curls.

Chocolate Peanut Pie

1 4-ounce package *regular* chocolate
    pudding mix
¼ cup peanut butter
1 2-ounce package dessert
    topping mix
1 *baked* 9-inch pastry shell
    (See *Pastry*)
2 tablespoons peanuts, chopped

Prepare pudding mix according to package directions, *except use only 1¾ cups milk.* Add small amount of hot pudding to peanut butter; beat till smooth. Beat into remaining pudding. Cover surface and cool, stirring once or twice. Prepare topping mix according to package directions; reserve ½ cup. Fold remaining topping into pudding. Pile into pastry shell; chill. Top with reserved dessert topping and nuts.